SGT. PEPPER'S LONELY HEARTS CLUB BAND

THE ALBUM, THE BEATLES AND THE WORLD IN 1967

Author's acknowledgement:
To Pat, who was with me then and is still with me now.
Thank you.

2017 First US edition

An Imagine Book

Published by Charlesbridge

85 Main Street

Watertown, MA 02472

www.imaginebooks.net

First published in 2017 by Carlton Books. An imprint of Carlton Publishing Group, 20 Mortimer Street, London W1T 3JW

Copyright © 2017 by Carlton Books Limited

Cataloging-in-Publication Data available upon request.

ISBN 978-1-62354-526-0

Printed in China

10 9 8 7 6 5 4 3 2 1

SGT. PEPPER'S LONELY HEARTS CLUB BAND

THE ALBUM, THE BEATLES AND THE WORLD IN 1967

BRIAN SOUTHALL

imagine!

CONTENTS

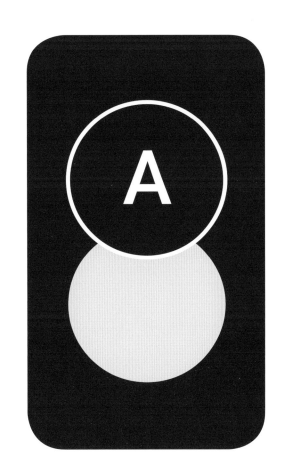

A-SIDE

B-SIDE

CONTENTS

FOREWORD

"It was 20 years ago today" – or so said Sgt Pepper. In fact, it is 50 years ago since the Beatles released the album that went on to change the world of music forever. This is a celebration of 1967...

Think back half a century if you can – you may not be old enough – and try to remember what was going on in your life. Throughout writing this book, I have had the pleasure of sharing memories with a host of people, including musicians, producers, composers, broadcasters, photographers, designers and fans who turned their minds back five decades to tell me what they remembered from the year when we experienced the "summer of love".

I was approaching 20 years of age when *Sgt. Pepper* came out in June 1967 and was employed at a local newspaper as a junior reporter. I'd dipped a toe in the world of pop music writing a column the paper had started in an attempt to receive free records.

When that worked, we branched out and began reviewing concerts and interviewing musical stars. My contribition to the column included giving Bob Dylan a thumbs-up for his 1965 show at London's Royal Albert Hall,

interviewing the Rolling Stones (with a very truculent Brian Jones) backstage at Southend Odeon and being told exclusively by Pete Townshend that the Who were so bored they were thinking of breaking up.

The column eventually folded, but nothing could dim my new-found love of popular music in all of its glorious forms. That, of course, included the Beatles, whose escapades I'd followed since 1962 and, as they went on to dominate the world, they shone through as unique talents who would never split up.

That was not to be the case, of course, but in the mid-sixties we didn't worry about musical differences or band bust-ups. The Beatles ruled the roost, even as their music developed to become more experimental and unshackled from any constraints and they evolved to produce a masterpiece suited to a time when psychedelia, love and peace were forever in the air.

Memories, at times, are hard to recall.

Nostalgia is hard to pin down. My wife and I have totally different memories as to where we were when – together then as a couple – we first heard the mighty sounds of *Sgt. Pepper*.

In my mind, we were all sitting around the record player in a schoolfriend's lounge – he had a big house with several large rooms. However, Pat, my wife, recalls that we were actually in the house of that same schoolmate's girlfriend. The fact that we heard the same album on the same day, but in houses 12 miles apart, is not important. What is relevant is that we both remember, clear as day, when we first heard the album's stunning tracks, 'Sgt. Pepper...', 'Within You Without You', 'Lucy In The Sky With Diamonds', 'When I'm Sixty-Four' and 'A Day In The Life'. I can't think of another album that I can pin down in the same way.

If you want any other reminders of what was happening in 1967 I can tell you that the cost of an average house in Britain was £3,840,

"The Beatles saved the world from boredom".

GEORGE HARRISON

petrol was 5s.2d a gallon and a new Mark II Ford Cortina would set you back £749. And, for those readers of a younger disposition, performers who were born 50 years ago this year include Faith Hill, Keith Urban, Vanilla Ice and the late Kurt Cobain.

Matching tie-pins and cuff-links were all the rage for the smarter man back then, while girls took to wearing mini-skirts – in "shock orange" or "switched-on pink" – with a metal chain belt. You could watch *The Prisoner, The Forsyte Saga, Doctor Who* (Patrick Troughton, at the time) *Z Cars* and *The Saint* on television

and the list of the year's greatest albums came from the Velvet Underground & Nico, the Doors, Love, Pink Floyd, Leonard Cohen, Jimi Hendrix and Cream.

The world's five biggest chart hits were calculated to be 'Whiter Shade Of Pale' (Procol Harum), 'I'm A Believer' (the Monkees), 'All You Need Is Love' (the Beatles), 'Light My Fire' (the Doors) and 'Strawberry Fields Forever' (the Beatles), which Sir Tim Rice describes as "a brilliant list – all five are just fantastic". And so they were. And always will be.

For those of us who were there in 1967 – and

no doubt for some who caught up with things a bit later – 1967 was a memorable year in history, and not just for the music. There were tragedies, scientific breakthroughs, wars and new laws, protests and major achievements in the arts, sport and politics.

You don't have to take my word for it as to how special things were back then. Even some of the Beatles were impressed...

Above: An anti-war demonstrator uses flower power on US military police at the Pentagon Building in October 1967.

" The year 1967 seems rather golden — it always seemed to be sunny and we wore far-out clothes and far-out sunglasses. Maybe calling it the summer of love was a bit too easy; but it was a golden summer. "

PAUL MCCARTNEY

" The summer of 1967 was the 'Summer of Love' for us. There was definitely a vibe — we could feel what was going on with our friends — and people who had similar goals in America. You could just pick up the vibes, man. "

GEORGE HARRISON

" As we went into 1967, one had the feeling that it was going to be quite a profound year. It was almost like the revolution that started in 1963 had really gathered pace and was going to lead to really big changes. "

DISC-JOCKEY JOHNNIE WALKER

" 1967 was a wild year in terms of music with the release of the Beatles' *Sgt. Pepper* and Jimi Hendrix's 'Purple Haze' and *Are You Experienced?*. "

SINGER BILLY IDOL (AGED 12 IN 1967)

" 1967 was a fantastic time. There was an awful lot going on in all areas. It was exciting to be part of it and it was momentous perhaps because everybody began to say this isn't a passing fad. This is our lives and culture for our youth and for a lot of other people. "

PHOTOGRAPHER GERED MANKOWITZ

" It was such a special time in England, that hazy, crazy summer of love. "

SINGER/SONGWRITER GRAHAM NASH

" The reception to *Sgt. Pepper* at Dartmouth College was emblematic of the culture change in 1967. The Beatles were unique in being both reflective of, and leading, our tastes. They were the cultural Mission Control. "

BROADCASTER AND JOURNALIST PAUL GAMBACCINI

" It was a nice year with the weather and the music. There were fun gatherings in the parks where people got together for a smoke and a good time. "

BEATLES FRIEND TONY BRAMWELL

" We used to go to all the clubs — Bag O'Nails, Ronnie Scott's, Ad-Lib — all the places in London and they were great. And you could get into all of them if you were a young pop star. "

SINGER/PRODUCER/MANAGER PETER ASHER

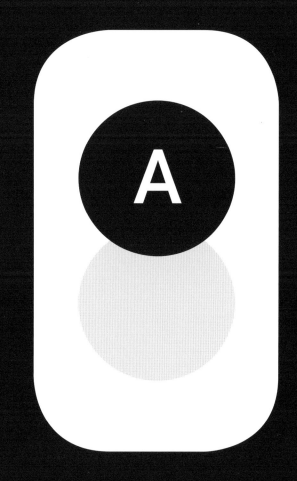

A-SIDE

THE BEATLES

The origins of the band dubbed the "most popular and influential pop group of all time" are not shrouded in any sort of mystery. John Lennon, Paul McCartney, George Harrison and Ringo Starr all came from Liverpool and served their music apprenticeship in clubs, pubs and theatres around the northwest of England in the late 1950s and early 1960s.

In March 1956, John Lennon became the founding member of a skiffle group called the Quarrymen. Before the year was out, Paul McCartney had been recruited to their ranks. The following February, Harrison was recruited as the fourth member (along with John "Duff" Lowe) and the group made their first ever record in a local Liverpool studio – a version of Buddy Holly's 'That'll Be The Day' coupled with the Harrison/McCartney song 'In Spite Of All The Danger' – at a cost of 17s 6d.

By the end of 1959, the trio of Lennon, McCartney and Harrison were calling themselves Johnny and the Moondogs and had made it through to the final round of the popular TV talent show Carroll Levis's *TV Star Search* in Manchester, but left for home before the final votes were cast. At the start of 1960, Stuart Sutcliffe joined as the bass player (sort of), which meant the group had four guitarists and no regular drummer.

However, for a tour backing singer Johnny Gentle, under the name the Silver Beetles, the fledgling group hired Tommy Moore as drummer until Pete Best was recruited on a permanent basis in August 1960, just in time for

their first trip to Germany. With the settled line-up of Lennon, McCartney, Harrison, Sutcliffe and Best, the band adopted the name the Beatles and settled into a mammoth session of over 100 shows in just over three months.

The rock band that grew out of a skiffle combo was now making progress with regular appearances in the clubs of Hamburg alongside a debut show at Liverpool's established Cavern Club and a record release. Their recording of 'My Bonnie', when they backed Tony Sheridan under the name the Beat Brothers, was released in Germany by Polydor and reached No.32 during a 12-week stay on the chart.

When a local Liverpool teenager Raymond Jones enquired about the record in Liverpool's NEMS record store, the shop's entrepreneurial owner Brian Epstein searched in vain for the disc. However, he became interested enough to go to the Cavern to see the Beatles perform live – now without Sutcliffe, who was living in Germany – at a lunchtime session on November 9, 1961. Then, a month before Epstein signed his first management deal with the group – dated February 1, 1962, for five years – the quartet travelled to London for an audition, which

Epstein had arranged at 11am on New Year's Day, 1962, at Decca's studios, West Hampstead.

In front of a small audience, they ran through 15 songs – including three written by Lennon and McCartney. Decca A&R man, Mike Smith, was present, but the group failed to win his approval or that of his boss, A&R chief Dick Rowe. The two executives instead opted to sign another group who had auditioned on the same day, Brian Poole and the Tremeloes. Epstein claimed that Rowe had told him, "We don't like your boys' sound. Groups are out: four-piece groups with guitar, particularly, are finished."

At this point, Epstein suggested to the group that they swap their leather outfits for a smarter look with matching suits and ties as he moved them out of scruffy halls and into venues with a stage and dressing rooms. In March 1962, the new smarter Beatles made their first ever radio appearance when they appeared in the BBC show *Teenager's Turn (Here We Go)*.

The Beatles, under the command of Epstein, were making progress but they still didn't have the one thing they all craved – a recording contract. Having been turned down by Decca, the group and their manager suffered further

setbacks when record labels EMI, Pye, Oriole and Philips all gave them a thumbs down. Undeterred, Epstein wandered into the giant HMV record store on London's Oxford Street, on May 8, to get the Beatles' Decca audition tape transferred onto an acetate. The tape engineer in the store was impressed by what he heard and directed Epstein upstairs to the offices of Sidney Coleman, director of music publisher Ardmore and Beechwood.

Coleman too was impressed and arranged a meeting the next day with Parlophone record producer George Martin, who listened to the tape and duly offered Epstein and the Beatles a

recording contract, which they signed at EMI's Manchester Square headquarters on June 4, 1962. It was a standard contract for the time and according to EMI managing director L.G. Wood, "Signing the Beatles was just like signing any other group."

It was a one-year deal with three one-year options and a final expiry date of June 5, 1966. The Beatles stood to earn 1d (.417 new pence) per double-sided disc and this would be split between the four group members and Brian Epstein. At 7pm on June 6, 1962, the Beatles assembled in Abbey Road Studios for their debut recording session under the direction of

Martin's assistant, Ron Richards. They recorded the songs, 'P.S. I Love You', 'Ask Me Why' and 'Bésame Mucho' and 'Love Me Do'.

By the time the Beatles returned to London for a second recording in Abbey Road on September 4, there had been a major change in the group's line-up. The decision was made to replace Best with Ringo Starr, from the rival group Rory Storm and the Hurricanes. Ringo made his debut at a Horticultural Society Dance at Hulme Hall, Port Sunlight, Birkenhead, on August 18, 1962.

During their session in September the Beatles were asked by Martin to record the song

'How Do You Do It' but insisted on also recording their own song 'Love Me Do', which was seen as a potential first single. A week later, Martin recorded the same song but this time hired session drummer Andy White to replace Starr on 'Love Me Do' while the new Beatles drummer played tambourine.

In between the two Abbey Road sessions, Epstein had signed another contract – this time for music publishing, which by his own admission was something, "I really had no idea what publishing meant." After their initial meeting in the HMV store, Coleman was keen to pick up the rights to the two songs set to be released on the first Beatles single for Ardmore and Beechwood. In return for the worldwide copyright to 'Love Me Do' and 'P.S. I Love You', the music publishers would pay Lennon and McCartney an advance of one shilling against royalties of 50 per cent from all record sales and 50 per cent from the monies collected by the Performing Rights Society (PRS).

With both recording and publishing contracts signed, the Beatles still had to wait until October 5 for the release of 'Love Me Do' on Parlophone. During the same month they made their TV debut, performing live at Granada TV's Manchester Studios for the programme *People and Places*. This was followed on October 28, with their first appearance at the mighty Liverpool Empire Theatre, where they supported Little Richard, Jet Harris and Craig Douglas.

1962 ended on one final high note as 'Love Me Do' peaked at No.17 in the UK singles chart, despite rumours that Brian Epstein had bought 10,000 copies to help it along the way.

On the back of their first UK tour, alongside Helen Shapiro and Kenny Lynch, the Beatles returned to Abbey Road studios on February 11, 1963, to complete their first album, *Please Please Me*, in one extraordinary session that ran from 10am until 10.45pm. The ten new songs were then accompanied by the two tracks from their debut single and the follow-up single, 'Please Please Me' and 'Ask Me Why', and the group's first album (rush-released on March 22) swept to the top of the UK chart in May.

The album replaced Cliff Richard's *Summer Holiday* and held the No.1 spot for the next 30 weeks before it was knocked off by... *With The Beatles* from December 1963 until May 1964. This meant that the Beatles' first two albums topped the UK chart for 51 weeks. Unheard of then – and now, come to think of it.

The quartet – now universally known as "the Mop Tops" or the "Fab Four" – also topped the British singles chart for the first time in 1963, although a mystery remains over which song has the distinction of being the Beatles' first No.1. 'Please Please Me' certainly reached the top spot in the charts operated by the leading music papers of the day – *Melody Maker*, *NME* and *Disc* – but became stuck at No.2 (behind Frank Ifield's 'The Wayward Wind') in what was seen as the "official" chart introduced by music industry magazine *Record Retailer* in January 1963.

But if 'Please Please Me' failed to become an official No.1, the follow-up 'From Me To You' – Lennon and McCartney took the title from *NME*'s reader's letters column, "From You To Us" – made up for it by holding the pole position for seven weeks and selling more than 650,000 copies. The Beatles were up and running and between 1963 and 1967 stacked up 11 consecutive UK number-one singles.

America too was now hot for a taste of the "Fab Four". After a cool reception from EMI's US sister label, Capitol, who passed on 'Love Me Do', 'Please Please Me', 'From Me To You' and 'She Loves You', allowing US independent labels Vee-Jay and Swan to release them, they finally went to No.1 in America with 'I Want To Hold Your Hand' in February 1964.

If Beatlemania was a phenomenon in Britain and Europe, the Americans managed to take it to another level as the Beatles achieved six US number ones in that same year and, at one time, held the top five positions on the official *Billboard* Hot 100 in one week in April 1964.

British beat groups were set to dominate proceedings on both sides of the Atlantic for the next couple of years, with the likes of Peter and Gordon, the Animals, Manfred Mann, Herman's Hermits, the Rolling Stones, the Dave Clark Five and the Troggs all reaching No.1 in the UK and US charts. And among those who failed to hit the top spot in America, but were still part of the British invasion spearheaded by the Beatles, were groups such as Gerry and the Pacemakers, Billy J Kramer and the Dakotas, the Searchers, Brian Poole and the Tremeloes, the Kinks, the Hollies and the Spencer Davis Group.

Throughout the "swingin' sixties", John, Paul, George and Ringo (their names could never come in any other order) continued to dominate the world of popular music in the face of stiff opposition. The likes of Elvis Presley, Cliff Richard, Roy Orbison, Tom Jones, Petula Clark, Dusty Springfield, Donovan and Georgie Fame were established solo artists at a time when Motown, America's newest sound from Detroit, arrived with the likes of the Supremes, Stevie Wonder, the Four Tops and the Temptations.

By 1966, the Beatles had played to full houses in theatres and stadiums all around the world, received countless gold discs and a host of international music awards and had been awarded MBEs (Member of the British Empire)

Left: With a background of balloons, Paul McCartney gets into the groove to record 'All You Need Is Love'.

Previous spread: The Beatles rehearse for the recording of 'All You Need Is Love' in Abbey Road Studios in June 1967.

by Queen Elizabeth II. But things were about to change. In May 1967, they made what would turn out to be their last UK concert performance at the *NME* Poll Winners Concert. Three months later, the band said goodbye to the road.

On August 29, the group assembled at San Francisco's Candlestick Park to give their final live performance. They played 11 songs to 25,000 fans. Nine years of touring and performing as the Quarrymen, Johnny and the Moondogs, the Silver Beetles and, finally, the Beatles, came to an end – after more than 1,400 shows.

Just as people had got over the shock of the Beatles retiring from live performances, their fans were in for another surprise in early 1967, when a new single – some thought the best the group ever released – failed to reach the No.1 spot in the UK and brought to an end their run of consecutive No.1 singles, which began back in May 1963. 'Penny Lane'/'Strawberry Fields Forever' only made it to No.2, held back by Engelbert Humperdinck's 'Release Me'.

Their "failure" was short-lived. The album that would go on to break all the rules, and most of the sales records, made an appearance in June 1967. *Sgt. Pepper's Lonely Hearts Club Band* was the most ambitious project the fab four from Liverpool had undertaken. For their pioneering efforts, they were rewarded with an album that swept to the top of the charts in both America (15 weeks) and Britain (27 weeks, spread between June and February 1968).

A month ahead of the release of *Sgt. Pepper*, EMI announced that the Beatles' total record sales worldwide were more than 200 million... with a whole lot more to come. However, tragedy would strike all their lives on August 27 when their long-time manager Brian Epstein was found dead at his London home.

After their ambitious film *Magical Mystery Tour* had been broadcast on BBC One – and mauled by TV critics – the Beatles moved into the final two years of the sixties in search of new opportunities. They opened (and closed)

a shop, launched a record label, and began working on individual music projects. But in May they once again assembled at Abbey Road Studios to start work on what would turn out to be the group's first and only double album. *The Beatles* (known as the *White Album* because of its distinctive plain white sleeve) was produced by a band in disarray and regarded as more of a collection of solo projects than a group effort.

For the second consecutive album, there were also no singles.

An album, with the working title *Get Back*, and released as *Let It Be*, began on January 22, 1969, but before the month was complete the Beatles had pulled yet another surprise – an unscheduled live appearance on the roof of their offices in London's upmarket Savile Row. Their 42-minute set – with Billy Preston on

Above: Ringo Starr tries his hand at the trumpet during a session in Abbey Road studios.

Right: George Martin (left) gives Paul McCartney a hand with his piano playing, circa 1967.

organ – was brought to an abrupt, but perhaps apt, end when the police arrived to deal with complaints by local residents about the noise.

Following Epstein's death, the Beatles never appointed anybody to succeed him, but in February 1969 American music publisher and artist manager Allen Klein was placed in charge as the group's business manager, with US lawyers Eastman and Eastman named general counsel a day later. The fact that one of the partners, Lee Eastman, was the father of McCartney's soon-to-be wife would play a vital role in the Beatles future business dealings.

Although *Let It Be* had been recorded during early 1969 it was not released until 1970 as another album – *Abbey Road* – was completed and issued first. With the famous cover shot of the Fab Four walking across the pedestrian crossing outside EMI's studios in St John's Wood, *Abbey Road* topped both the UK and US charts. For George Martin it marked the end of a seven-year relationship and he remarked, "It was the last thing they ever did together, so *Abbey Road* has a special place for me."

It may not have been their final recording, but the Beatles' final release was the long-awaited *Let It Be* album and it appeared with changes made to McCartney's song, 'The Long And Winding Road', by the producer Phil Spector ... without any consultation with its composer. Even before this musical insult, the rift between McCartney and his three fellow Beatles had begun to grow wider. McCartney was not in favour of Allen Klein representing him or the band, and the other three members in turn did not want Paul's father-in-law, Lee Eastman, running their affairs. After eight years as the world's most successful group, it was all heading towards a messy conclusion.

As if to emphasize his displeasure with the situation, McCartney released his debut solo album, *McCartney*, in April 1970, a couple of weeks before the release of the final Beatles album. And, while that album reached the No.1 spot in America ahead of *Let It Be*, his band's record did eventually replace him on top of the chart. Meanwhile, in the UK, the new solo Beatle had to be content with the No.2 chart position behind *Let It Be*, the group's eleventh No.1.

The release of his new album coincided with McCartney issuing a press release in which he answered his own questions:

Q) Is your break with the Beatles temporary or permanent, due to personal differences or musical ones?

A) Personal differences. Business differences. Musical differences. But, most of all, because I have a better time with my family. Temporary or permanent? I don't know.

Q) Is it true that neither Allen Klein nor ABCK [Klein's company] have been, or will be, in any way involved in the production, manufacturing, distribution or promotion of this new album?

A) Not if I can help it.

McCartney also answered a journalist who asked if he foresaw a time when he might write songs with Lennon again, with a simple "No".

If the break-up of the Beatles began back in 1969 when Klein and Eastman appeared on opposite sides of the ring, the final round was played out in the Chancery Division of the High Court on the very last day of 1970. It was here that McCartney filed suit against the rest of the group to dissolve the Beatles and Co. partnership that had been set up in 1967. At the same time, he also cut all ties with Klein.

In March 1971, a High Court judge found in favour of McCartney and appointed a receiver to oversee the group's affairs. However, it would

be another four years, in January 1975, before the four ex-Beatles got together to formally dissolve their partnership.

Maybe the quartet knew exactly what lay in store for them when a track they recorded on July 23, 1969, became the last song on the final album ever recorded by the group. It was called 'The End'. And, in the end, with this declarative statement of closure, the Beatles were no more.

Above: George Harrison finds time for a break in Plymouth during the Beatles' Magical Mystery Tour.

Left: John Lennon (left) and Paul McCartney arrive back from their holiday in Greece in July 1967.

JOHN LENNON

Who was the leader of the Beatles? For most people, including fellow group member George Harrison, it was John Lennon. He was instrumental in founding the Quarrymen and asking Paul McCartney into the group, even though Lennon had some reservations about his new recruit: "I'd been the kingpin up to then. I'd have to keep him in line."

Lennon's next decision was to rename the group the Beetles, in honour of Buddy Holly's backing group the Crickets, before opting for Long John Silver and the Beetles.

The fact that the group then became the Silver Beetles before eventually settling on the Beatles has gone down in history as Lennon's idea. While nobody in the group has ever ultimately claimed the credit, Lennon, in one of his early nonsense verses, wrote, "Beatles, how did the name arrive? So, we will tell you. It came in a vision – a man appeared on a flaming pie and said unto them, 'From this day on you are Beatles with an A' – 'Thank you, Mister Man,' they said, thanking him."

According to the group's long-time friend Tony Bramwell, John Lennon "always saw himself as the nominal leader of the group." He certainly led the Quarrymen out of skiffle and into rock 'n' roll, thanks to his love of American music in the 1950s.

Like every other teenager, Lennon was listening to the music of Elvis Presley, Eddie Cochran, Carl Perkins, Little Richard, Gene Vincent and Buddy Holly and he became influenced in a big way. "Once I heard it and got into it, that was life. I thought of nothing else but rock 'n' roll."

In the early and mid-sixties, Lennon was the dominating force in the group – writing or singing most of the hits – until McCartney began to make his mark. "There was a little competition between Paul and me as to who got the A-side. It wasn't resentment, but it was competition," he explained.

Lennon's upbringing in Liverpool was not in a conventional suburban family. In 1940, his father left home before Lennon was born, leaving his mother Julia to cope as a single parent. Eventually, John moved in with his aunt and uncle, Mimi and George Smith, and spent the rest of childhood and teenage years at their house in Menlove Avenue. In 1958, when Lennon was 17, his mother Julia was killed by a hit-and-run driver and, in his own words, Lennon admitted he was traumatized. "It was the worst thing that ever happened to me. It just absolutely made me very, very bitter. The chip on my shoulder that I had as a youth got really big then. Being a teenager and a rock 'n' roller and an art student and my mother being killed, just when I was re-establishing a relationship with her."

In his book *Lennon*, Ray Coleman, a music journalist close to the Beatles throughout the sixties, described the singer as "brilliant, generous, sensitive yet abrasive, tough and sarcastic".

In his formative years, it wasn't just music that appealed to Lennon, who failed academically but developed a fascination for art and drawing. In 1964, Lennon produced his first book of verse, rhymes and drawings, entitled *In His Own Write*. "When the group started going out on the road, I used to take out my typewriter after the show and just tap away."

The book sold more than 100,000 copies and turned Lennon into a bestselling author. His follow-up, *A Spaniard in the Works*, published a year later, was another bestseller.

In 1966, a remark Lennon made to British journalist Maureen Cleave, that the Beatles were "more popular than Jesus", erupted into a controversy in America as the group's records were burned and banned by those who considered it a dig at Christianity. After an awkward public apology, the band were allowed to continue to tour the USA.

But, soon after, they abandoned life on the road, and went into the studio to create some of the most experimental music of the decade, and gradually Lennon moved on from being a Beatle. Following the break-up of his marriage to art college sweetheart Cynthia, in 1968, he met and married Japanese avant-garde artist Yoko Ono. They began producing controversial albums alongside a campaign for peace that involved 'bed-ins' and 'bag-ins'.

Thankfully, Lennon still knew how to write and produce hit records and solo albums. *Imagine* (1971), *Some Time in New York City* (1972) and *Walls and Bridges* (1974) kept him at the forefront of the music scene.

While John Lennon was the only one of the Beatles I never met during my time at EMI – and he was the one I most wanted to meet – I received several postcards and telexes from him when he was living in New York. He was a big fan of postcards and sent them to family and friends, journalists and record company people, with suggestions about how his records should be marketed and distributed.

John Lennon was tragically murdered on December 8, 1980, but the contribution he made during his lifetime lives on in his music, his art and his quest for peace and freedom of speech. He is remembered as a poet, artist, wit and philosopher.

Right: John Lennon poses at the launch party for *Sgt. Pepper* in May 1967.

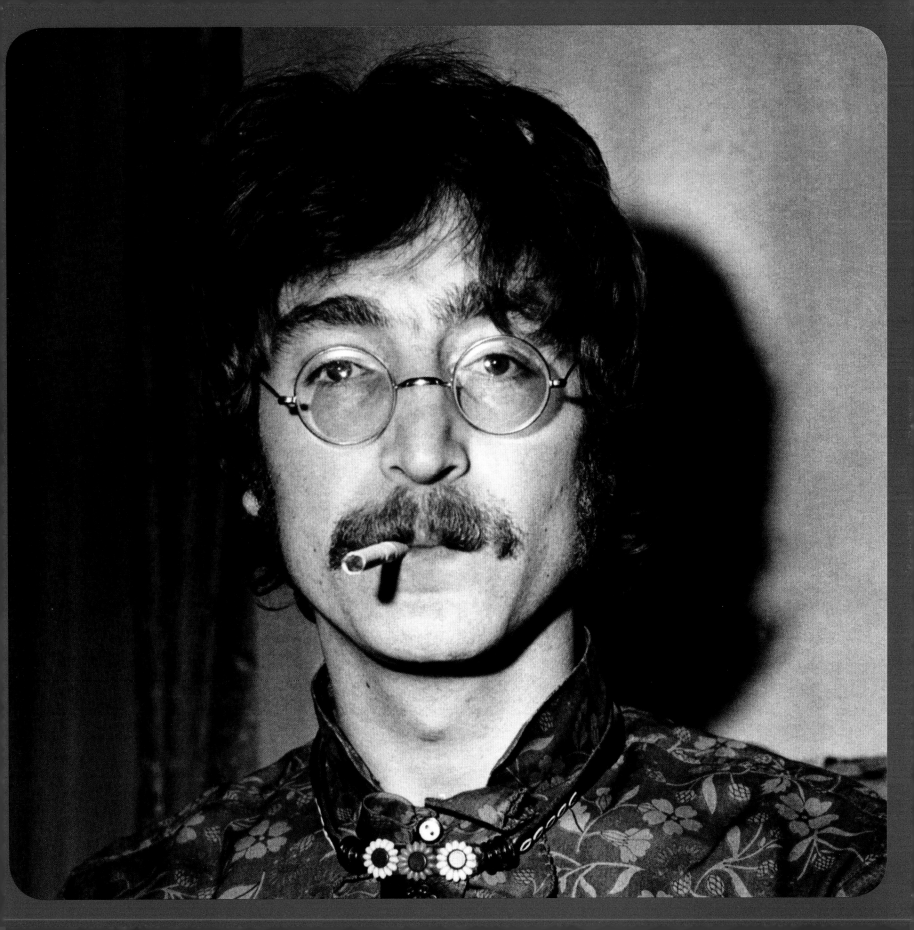

PAUL MCCARTNEY

Paul McCartney and John Lennon both loved rock 'n' roll. And even before they got to know each other as teenagers in Liverpool they were listening to the same records by the same American musicians.

But it was McCartney's ability to play the guitar that brought him to the attention of the leader of the Quarrymen on the afternoon of July 6, 1957, when the group had finished playing at a garden fête at St Peter's Church, Woolton, Liverpool. "We talked after the show and I saw he had talent," recalled Lennon. "I was very impressed by Paul playing 'Twenty Flight Rock'. He could obviously play the guitar."

McCartney's ability to play Eddie Cochran's song, at age fifteen, changed his life for ever, with him once exclaiming, "That's what got me into the Beatles."

Often meeting at McCartney's home at 20 Forthlin Road in the Liverpool district of Allerton, the two youngsters "bunked off" school and art college to play acoustic guitar and work on composing songs that McCartney had written in an exercise book under the heading, "Another Lennon/McCartney original". Among the first songs the pair wrote in the front room of the small terraced house were 'I Saw Her Standing There' and 'Love Me Do'.

Written in the late 1950s, those two songs would both figure prominently when the Beatles began releasing records. 'Love Me Do' was chosen as the group's first single in October 1962 while 'I Saw Her Standing There' became the opening track on their debut album *Please Please Me*. And back then, despite McCartney's jottings in his school book, both were credited as being written by McCartney-Lennon.

Geoff Emerick, an engineer at Abbey Road Studios, who began working with the Beatles in February 1963, remembers McCartney as the "most friendly and engaging" of the four young Liverpudlians. He also spotted something else: "I had the impression he was the leader of the group."

McCartney was also, according to Tony Bramwell, a man who delighted in the compliments that were directed at the Beatles. After *The Times* compared the Beatles to Ludwig van Beethoven, McCartney took to referring to the composer as "Beathoven" and became inspired to come up with a new sound: "He would sit in the music room at the top of his London house and use some of the electronic gadgetry he had bought and create a sound – layers of Beatles overlaid on Beethoven."

Post-1967, as McCartney drifted away from Lennon, their creative partnership also suffered with each of them writing more and more songs on their own. By the time the Beatles came to produce their final three albums – *The Beatles*, *Abbey Road* and *Let It Be* – it was obvious to everyone that this was not a group working together in harmony.

Despite this, all compositions created under the banner of the Northern Songs publishing company were still credited to Lennon-McCartney. This decision was made in 1963 – after the original credit of McCartney-Lennon had appeared – and McCartney was, by his own admission, not best pleased. When he asked why the names were being reversed he was told that it sounded better. His reply was "not to me it doesn't," but he obviously lost the fight.

There were, however, bigger battles to come for the four Beatles as, in the aftermath of Epstein's death, they chose to follow very different paths, creatively, personally, and professionally. After instigating the break-up of the band, McCartney also took to life after the

Beatles with renewed enthusiasm, producing a canon of work that only served to add to his reputation as pop music's most prolific singer-songwriter.

The accomplishments are legendary. His song 'Yesterday' is the most recorded song in history, his earnings have made him the wealthiest man in British music, he is the recipient of a record number of Ivor Novello Awards, is a Grammy Lifetime Achievement Award winner and was awarded a knighthood in 1997.

When I was at EMI, I worked with McCartney occasionally from the mid-1970s onwards. During those years, he was an irregular visitor to the offices, but he was always as charming as his public persona – except for when we were discussing forthcoming releases or the promotion or marketing of his records. Because he had achieved everything there was to achieve in music, he wasn't a man you would argue with over the choice of singles, artwork design or TV and radio promotion. "Once you have conquered the world, nothing surprises you," he has said.

To this day, Paul McCartney continues to record and release music, and perform all over the world. In 1967, McCartney reflected on his former band's success, and their desire for revolution and evolution: "Each of us still has our basic role in the group, but we always appear to be changing because we don't conform. It's this not conforming and wanting to do something different which keeps our music different. I could sit back now and be a company director until I'm 70, but I wouldn't learn as much as I would by trying new things".

Left: Paul McCartney hits 25 at his St John's Wood home, June 1967.

A

GEORGE HARRISON

George Harrison began his career as a guitarist when he was around 13 years old, with a second-hand instrument he bought from a schoolmate with money – £3 10s – his mum gave him. It may have been a "real cheapo horrible little guitar", but it served a useful purpose when he met a fellow student on the bus.

Both Harrison and Paul McCartney travelled together to Liverpool Institute High School for Boys, but, even though they were on the same bus, and dressed in the same uniform, they didn't know each other. McCartney was a year older than Harrison but once they found out that they shared a love of music – "I discovered that he had a trumpet and he found out that I had a guitar" – a bond was struck.

In a similar fashion to McCartney impressing Lennon with his guitar skills, Harrison also displayed his virtuoso abilities to McCartney and Lennon on the top deck of an empty bus. He played Bill Justis's 'Raunchy'. It was left to Lennon to decide whether George could join the Quarrymen. "We asked him to join because he knew more chords, a lot more than we knew," said Lennon.

As the group switched from being the Silver Beetles to simply the Beatles, and while Lennon and McCartney were honing their skills as songwriters, Harrison studied guitar manuals and played along with records in an effort to improve his playing. "Someone gave me a Chet Atkins album and I started to try and figure out tunes with different chords."

The Beatles continued to expand their horizons and in addition to being regulars on the UK's northwest club scene and making their first appearances in two clubs in Hamburg, they had ventured south to play in Aldershot and to give their first-ever London gig – at the Blue Gardenia Club in Soho. Word was spreading and Harrison could see a dream coming true. "I wanted to be a

musician and when the group got together we all had an amazing, positive feeling about being in the band full-time," he said.

Alongside the acerbic wit of John's and Paul's tactful remarks, Harrison was seen as the Beatle with the driest sense of humour. The staff present at Abbey Road Studios on the day the Beatles came in for their audition were taken by a remark the young guitarist made to George Martin. The producer had given the group a stern talking to about their performance when, according to engineer Norman Smith, he asked them if there was anything they didn't like. "George Harrison looked up and said to George Martin, 'I don't like your tie.' That was it for me. We had to sign them for their wit."

But there was one major component lacking in Harrison's life as a Beatle – the opportunity to contribute his songs. While Lennon and McCartney were the established songwriting team, Harrison had his own ambitions as a composer and, in 1963, he was rewarded when 'Don't Bother Me' appeared on their second album, *With the Beatles*.

However, he would have to wait until the group's fifth album to get another chance when two songs – 'I Need You' and 'You Like Me Too Much' – were included on *Help!*. Harrison was also reluctant to assign his songs to Northern Songs – the publishing company created by Brian Epstein, Lennon, McCartney and Dick James – but they were put there anyway. "Brian Epstein was in cahoots with Dick James," was Harrison's view.

George also believed that the songs he was writing were the equal of those of his two bandmates, but still he was frustrated by the lack of opportunity. "Sometimes I had songs that were better than some of their songs and we'd have to record maybe eight of theirs before they'd listen to one of mine."

Despite having the lowest profile of all the Beatles, Harrison was the first to experiment on his own. In 1968, he composed music for the film *Wonderwall* while his experimental album *Electronic Sound* came out in 1969, the same year 'Something' was released as a Beatles A-side – the first non-Lennon-McCartney composition to be released as a single.

Harrison became the first solo Beatle to achieve a No.1 album – *All Things Must Pass* – and to top the single charts, with 'My Sweet Lord'. He recorded these pieces of music when he was deeply committed to Eastern culture, philosophy and the Hare Krishna movement, while also pursuing his interest in film producing and motor racing.

George Harrison died of cancer on November 29, 2001. I have one lasting memory of a meeting with George, in 1975, when we met to discuss his *Extra Texture (Read All About It)* album. I was in his London office, before Harrison, his driver and I went on to Manchester Square for the meeting. When we got out of the car Harrison said he was going to the bathroom and I made my way up to the first floor of the EMI offices – where the Beatles had been photographed for the *Please Please Me* album cover – and met the company's managing director on the landing. He had been told that Harrison had arrived and was anxious to meet the ex-Beatle but instead met me – complete with shoulder-length hair and a beard. "Hello, George," he said. "How is it going without the others?" I told him I was the head of his own EMI press office and he replied, "That's good," before walking off to join the meeting.

When I told George, he thought it was hilarious and some years later a director of Apple told me Harrison had gone back and related the whole story to all the people in the office.

Right: George Harrison in his finest gear for recording 'All You Need Is Love'.

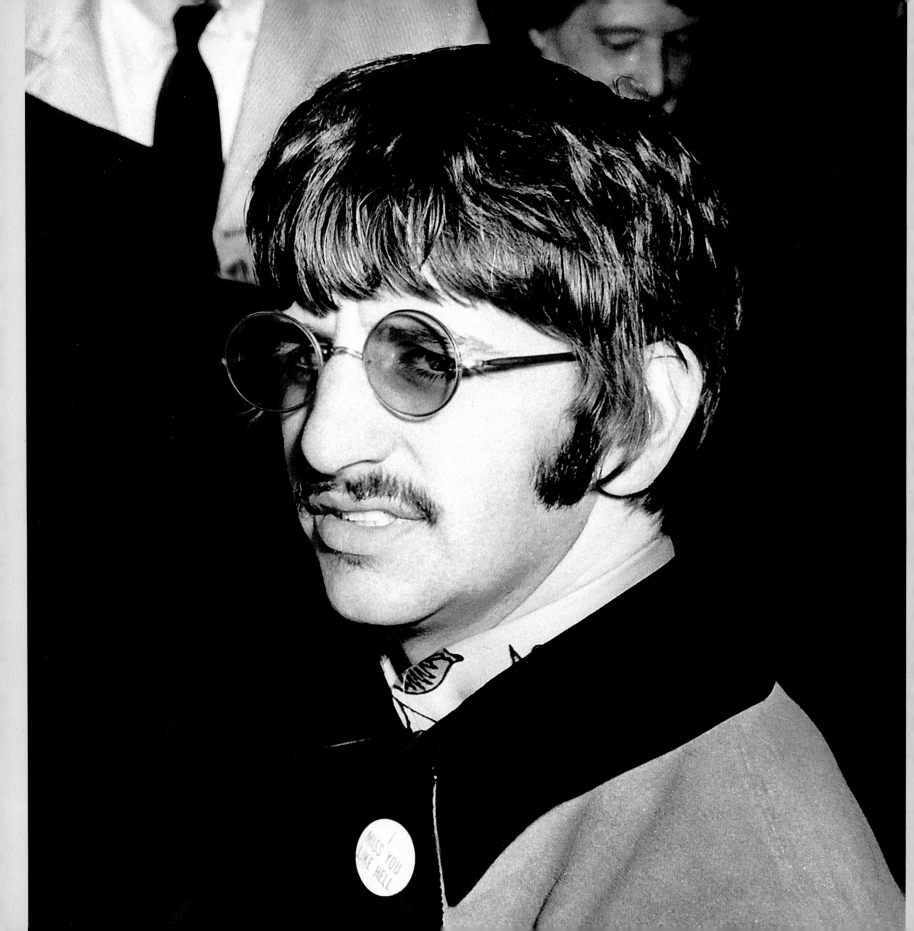

RINGO STARR

Richard Starkey's family clubbed together to raise the £13 it cost to buy him his first proper drum kit. The youngster was overjoyed. "It wasn't just a drum but drums: a snare, a bass drum, a hi-hat, one little tom-tom a top cymbal and a bass-drum pedal." He was so excited he even went and had lessons (only three) before settling into a routine of practising in his bedroom at home in Admiral Grove, Liverpool.

Working as an engineer during the day and playing the drums in the evening, Starkey moved through a host of local Liverpool groups, starting out with the Eddie Clayton Skiffle Group before moving on to the Darktown Skiffle Group and then, in 1959, Al Caldwell's Texans. When rock 'n' roll took over from skiffle, the Texans became Rory Storm and the Hurricanes.

During a summer season residency at Butlin's holiday camp in Pwllheli, Wales, Storm decided the band's drummer should become Ringo Starr, and have his own 'Ringo Starrtime' spot when, for the first time, Ringo would sing 'Boys' and 'You're Sixteen'. As Liverpool, and Hamburg's most popular act on the club scene at the time, Storm and the Hurricanes topped the bill in Hamburg's Kaiserkeller Club, with support from a new Liverpool band, the Beatles.

It was during another summer season at Butlin's, this time in Skegness, that John Lennon and Paul McCartney turned up and offered Starr £25 a week to join their group as a replacement for Pete Best. While George Martin had expressed some concerns about Best as a qualified drummer, the three other Beatles were becoming disenchanted for other reasons. "It was a personality thing," said McCartney. "He was different to the rest of us, not so studenty."

It was left to Brian Epstein to sack Best, and while Starr prepared to make his debut as an official Beatle in August 1962, the local Best fan club protested over the sacking of their hero.

However, before the Beatles returned to Abbey Road Studios a month later, their new drummer had been told to shave off his beard and change his hairstyle.

Despite several fans suggesting that Starr became "the luckiest man in the world" when he sat in the hot seat as the Beatles' drummer, he also became the senior member of the group. Tony Bramwell, whose childhood friendship with Harrison led him to work for Epstein in his NEMS business, explains what Starr brought to the Beatles dynamic. "He was laid back and easy to get on with. He was funny and outgoing and fitted in. And he was older than the others and was held in awe."

In his days with Storm, Starr had his own spot. With the Beatles he was again given the chance on stage, and on record, to contribute to the group's performances, although he got to perform just four songs as lead vocalist – 'Boys', 'Honey Don't', 'I Wanna Be Your Man' and 'Act Naturally' – during their live shows.

Ringo had even fewer opportunities than George Harrison to contribute any of his own material, with just two solo efforts, 'Don't Pass Me By' and 'Octopus's Garden', making it onto albums, though he was credited as a co-writer with the other Beatles on 'Flying', 'Dig It' and 'Christmas Time (Is Here Again)'.

Despite being last to join the Beatles, Starr, perhaps surprisingly, was the first to leave when he quit in August 1968 during a recording session for the *White Album*. At a time when relationships between all the boys were strained, waiting for hours for the other three to turn up finally took its toll and the drummer walked out on the sessions. Everyone who witnessed was sworn to secrecy. Starr returned after a few days to find the studio and his drum kit decorated with flowers.

Interestingly, as the Beatles became embroiled in more and more disagreements, it was Starr who stepped in as peacemaker; the group chose his home as the place for meetings aimed at sorting out their differences. Whether Starr could predict where the Beatles were headed or not, he decided to step out from behind his drum kit in 1968 to appear as a Mexican gardener in the film *Candy* before acting alongside Peter Sellers in the film *The Magic Christian*.

In 1970, Ringo released his first solo album, *Sentimental Journey*, quickly following it up, later that year, with *Beaucoups of Blues*. Since the formal breaking up of the Beatles, Starr has continued to record and tour regularly with his All-Starr Band.

Ringo was undoubtedly the funniest Beatle. When he visited EMI's offices in the 1970s, he came across as serious and reserved. Until, that is, he had the opportunity to throw in a witty quip. The group's press officer during their Apple days, Derek Taylor, once told me how he remembered each of the Beatles during their time in their office and, according to him, Starr "came in, told three or four jokes and then went home again".

Questions about Starr's ability as a drummer have continued long after the demise of the Beatles but the "world's wealthiest drummer" has his devoted fans. In 2011, readers of *Rolling Stone* magazine voted Ringo the fifth best drummer of all-time, behind Dave Grohl, Neil Peart, Keith Moon and John Bonham. Singer-songwriter Harry Nilsson once told me, with no uncertainty, that "Ringo is the best back-beat drummer in the world."

Left: Ringo Starr leaving hospital after visiting his new son Jason and wife Maureen in August 1967.

BRIAN EPSTEIN

Brian Epstein and George Martin, the two men regularly referred to as the "fifth Beatle", may have been born 12 years apart, in cities at opposite ends of England, but from the time they first met the group, both showed a love and dedication for them that knew no bounds. While neither Brian nor George ever publicly claimed the title of "fifth Beatle", the contribution they made to the success of the group is clear for all to see – one as manager, protector and ambassador, the other as producer, collaborator and adviser.

Brian Epstein was born in Liverpool on September 19, 1934, and despite his early protestations he was destined to join the family's furniture store business. Brian left school with ambitions of being a dress designer but, after being discharged from the Royal Army Service, he found himself in the Hoylake branch of the family business.

Homosexuality was illegal in Britain in the late 1950s and Epstein's youth was blighted by stories of his attempting to pick up men in public toilets. Brian's father opened a NEMS (North East Music Stores) branch in Great Charlotte Street when his son was 23 years old. Brian was put in charge of the ground-floor record department. When his father opened a bigger store in Whitechapel, 'Mr Brian' – as he was known to his staff – oversaw a new successful business and, for the first time, began to take an active interest in pop music. At a concert featuring Marty Wilde and Billy Fury, at the Liverpool Empire in 1958, Epstein secured a meeting with London-based pop impresario Larry Parnes, who introduced the young store manager to his British roster of rock 'n' roll stars.

In 1961, Epstein first became aware of the Beatles and ventured up to the Cavern Club to see them. He gradually developed a relationship with Lennon, McCartney, Harrison and Best, which resulted in the group signing a contract employing Epstein as the manager of the Beatles. The contract stipulated that he was to earn 10 per cent of any income up to £1,500 and 15 per cent on anything above that.

As one of the largest record stores in the northwest of England, NEMS had some clout with record companies, but not enough, it appears, to engineer Epstein's group a contract, although EMI managing director L.G. Wood once informed me that he thought Epstein's standing as a major retailer – and a guest of EMI at music industry dinners – played a significant part in the company eventually signing the Beatles.

To the Beatles, Epstein was a successful businessman, so they were happy to leave their affairs in his hands. "We had complete faith in him when he was runnin' us," observed Lennon. "To us, he was the expert. Anybody who had a shop must be all right. He went around charmin' everybody."

After Martin had offered Epstein and his charges a recording contract at Parlophone, Epstein then, after a one-off deal with music publisher Ardmore and Beechwood, set up Northern Songs, a new music publishing company, together with Dick James, to manage the songs written by the Beatles' two principle writers.

Under the deal, James owned half the company with the other 50 per cent being shared by Epstein, Lennon and McCartney. Years later, McCartney explained that it was a deal that he and Lennon were not entirely happy with. "John and I were taken for a ride. We signed everything away one morning. We didn't understand what it was."

At the time, however, all the members of the group trusted Epstein, who had smartened and sharpened their image, improved the quality of their bookings, increased their earnings and got them into the big-time world of pop. But that was where his influence ended as the Beatles kept their music-making separate from Epstein's deal-making. When Epstein once suggested to Lennon that something he had sung in the studio was not "quite right", the singer barked back at him, "You stick to your percentages, Brian. We'll look after the music."

After Epstein had established NEMS Enterprises – which involved the management of acts such as Gerry and the Pacemakers, Billy J Kramer and the Dakotas and Cilla Black, and the acquisition of the Saville Theatre in April 1965 – Epstein began re-negotiating the Beatles' second deal with EMI in 1965. It was intended to replace the initial agreement that was due to expire in June 1966. "I had quite a good relationship with Brian, but he could still be pig-headed and difficult over some things," recounts EMI's Wood. "He always wanted a contract that was different because he said his boys were 'out of the ordinary'." Ultimately, Epstein's stubbornness won a deal that secured the Beatles a 6.5 per cent royalty based on the retail price (instead of dealer price) of their records for the first 100,000 singles sales and first 30,000 albums, which increased to 10 per cent on additional sales.

It's interesting to note that at that time in the mid-1960s the negotiations involved only Wood and Epstein – "the lawyers came in when we had agreed everything," said Wood. The new deal was for nine years, with the Beatles committing themselves to record for only four years and make no more than 70 single sides. "Seventy sides in four years was not something we got terribly excited about," was Wood's later observation on the deal, which did not take effect until January 1967, leaving the Beatles without a contract for more than six months, from mid-1966.

Epstein's own deal as manager of the Beatles was due to expire at the end of 1967 and there

Right: October 1963 and Brian Epstein, manager of the Beatles, finds time to enjoy a cuppa in the NEMS office.

was some talk that the group were looking for a management change, despite Epstein telling *Melody Maker*'s Mike Hennessey in August 1967, "I am certain that they will not agree to be managed by anyone else." However, speaking in 1982, McCartney commented: "Brian's reign was ending. To begin with we needed the man in the Ford Zodiac to get us recording contracts and to make sure we wore the right clothes. But by 1967 a lot of things were escaping his grasp."

Epstein had certainly let the Beatles down over an American merchandising deal with a company called Seltaeb (Beatles, backwards), which gave NEMS and the Beatles just 10 per cent of the income, compared with 90 per cent to the US company. But still the music industry knew Epstein to be an honest and hard-working

manager who only had the Beatles best interests at heart. Certainly, Pete Brown, who worked at NEMS and Apple from 1957 to 1970, has no doubts about his employer's integrity. "History has shown that Epstein was probably one of the most honest managers in the industry, although he was naïve in the sense that everything was new to him."

On August 27, 1967, the world awoke to the news that Epstein, aged just 32, was dead. He was found on the bed in his Chapel Street home in London. The coroner's verdict revealed that he died as a result of an accidental overdose of the barbiturate, Carbitral. The *New York Times* called Epstein "the man who revolutionized pop music in our time". The Beatles were in Bangor, North Wales, studying

transcendental meditation with Maharishi Mahesh Yogi when news of the death broke. The band were recorded leaving the college, and were visibly shocked by the news. According to EMI chairman Sir Joseph Lockwood, with Epstein gone, there was nobody "to comfort them and tell them how to handle things". Speaking for the group, McCartney announced: "No one could possibly replace Brian." In the aftermath, various contenders for the job of looking after the Beatles' affairs appeared on the horizon including two directors of NEMS – music agent Vic Lewis and manager and entrepreneur Robert Stigwood. However, the Beatles opted to look after their own affairs, which for the next three years they would do with varying degrees of success.

GEORGE MARTIN

George Martin was born in London on January 3, 1926. After serving in the Fleet Air Arm of the Royal Navy, he attended the Guildhall School of Music for three years before joining the BBC, working in their Music Library.

When he joined EMI in 1950, Martin, by his own admission, was entering unknown territory. "I didn't even know what EMI stood for. I only took the job as a stop gap because I really wanted to be a pianist," he once told me. As assistant to the head of Parlophone label, Oscar Preuss, Martin quickly realized where Parlophone ranked in importance at EMI. "Columbia and HMV were the chief protagonists. Parlophone was on the side-lines. It was the weakest of the labels," was his assessment.

When he succeeded Preuss as Artists and Repertoire Manager, Martin added acts such as Peter Ustinov, Peter Sellers, Humphrey Lyttelton, Johnny Dankworth and Flanders and Swann to the roster, plus a singer called Dick James whose TV theme song of *The Adventures of Robin Hood* earned Martin a top ten hit in 1956.

Earning £1,100 per annum, Martin continued to produce hits from the likes of the King Brothers, Peter Sellers and Sophia Loren and Charlie Drake, before new acts arrived including Adam Faith, Matt Monro and the Temperance Seven – who gave the label its first ever number one with 'You're Driving Me Crazy'.

By 1962, pop was big business and while EMI boasted of Cliff Richard and the Shadows, Johnny Kidd and the Pirates, Helen Shapiro, John Leyton and Danny Williams on their Columbia and HMV imprints, Martin's Parlophone was on the hunt for new talent. Then came a meeting with a record shop owner who managed a four-piece group.

When the Beatles signed to Parlophone it meant that they would become regular visitors

to EMI's Abbey Road Studios, where they worked regularly with Martin's production team of Norman Smith and Geoff Emerick. "We were not allowed to touch the desk or anything else in those early days," says McCartney. "It was all very formal and in our early photos we have all got suits and ties on and so have George and Geoff."

Having signed the Beatles, Martin and his team then found themselves inundated with new talent as the "beat boom" began to explode. Much of it came from Epstein, whose stable of acts were all required to record at Abbey Road Studios.

At the start of their recording career the Beatles were studio novices and Martin's experience and contribution was an essential part of getting the band to sound just right. "In the early days, I can remember what George Martin did. He would translate. If Paul wanted to use violins he would translate it for him," said Lennon in a 1971 interview for *Rolling Stone*.

Throughout the 1960s Martin and the Beatles remained conjoined, even though Martin left EMI in 1965 when the company refused to reward him for his work with the Beatles, work that had produced huge earnings for the company. Martin went solo, and founded AIR Studios (Associated Independent Recording) and took Abbey Road stalwarts Peter Sullivan, John Burgess and Ron Richards with him.

Despite this move, Martin continued to work with the Beatles at Abbey Road, although by now the group were keen to be more involved in the recording and production of their music. "We started to take over," said McCartney, but this "takeover" still required Martin to be on

hand as the arranger, musician and producer who could "translate" the group's dreams and turn them into realities.

But all that changed with *Let It Be*.

The recordings the Beatles had made for the abandoned *Get Back* project were handed to legendary American producer Phil Spector. The man who produced the Ronettes, and Ike and Tina Turner's biggest hits was introduced to the Beatles by their new business manager Allen Klein but, as George Harrison, commented, "I was all for the idea of getting Phil involved."

However, when Spector famously altered McCartney's song 'Let It Be' without telling the composer and the original producer, they were both far from happy. "I didn't like Phil Spector's 'Let It Be' at all," remembered Martin, who added, "... and I resented him for it, because to me it was tawdry."

For McCartney, Spector's production represented unwarranted and unnecessary interference. His reaction to the song's new sound was blunt: "It sounded terrible." Fortunately, the story of Martin and the Beatles did not end with 'Let It Be' and the release of *Abbey Road* in September 1969 proved to be a fitting finale to a studio partnership that stretched back more than seven years.

Even after the Beatles imploded, and went their separate ways, Martin continued to work on anthologies, various reissues and compilations of the music he had helped to create. However, when McCartney, Harrison and Starr reunited in 1995 to work on Lennon's demo tapes of 'Free As A Bird' and 'Real Love', Martin had suffered significant hearing loss, and handed the project over to ELO's

Jeff Lynne to produce.

In 1996, the same year he was knighted by Queen Elizabeth II for his contribution to music, and at the age of 70, Martin announced his retirement from recording, citing his age and deafness. On March 8, 2016, at the grand age of 90, Sir George Martin died at his home in Wiltshire. His death was announced to the world by Ringo Starr, and Paul McCartney paid moving tribute to him: "He was a true gentleman and like a second father to me. If anyone earned the title of the fifth Beatle it was George."

When I joined EMI, Martin had already created his AIR studio complex, but when I began to write the official history of Abbey Road Studios in 1981 nobody could have been more helpful. I spent hours in the company of George, and his wife Judy, who was a secretary at Parlophone when he joined, and I had the pleasure of meeting them both regularly at industry events or award shows.

However, there is one incident, a memory about George, that I will never forget. Standing on the street outside EMI's Manchester Square offices one afternoon, I heard this cry of "Brian, Brian over here." When I turned around it was George Martin, calling me over to join him. The man who made the Beatles records recognized me and wanted to chat.

Years later, I was at Royal Festival Hall for a Phil Collins Big Band concert. During the interval, I found myself standing next to George in the toilets. "Enjoying the show?" I asked. "Tremendous fun!" he exclaimed, before adding, "Mind you, I'm as deaf as a post. It probably helps."

SGT. PEPPER: SIDE ONE

According to Brian Wilson, the musical force behind the Beach Boys, there is a creative strand which unites the Beatles' sixth album, *Rubber Soul,* with his own group's most acclaimed release, *Pet Sounds*. It is a link that would inspire the writing and recording of *Sgt. Pepper's Lonely Hearts Club Band.*

Above: *Pet Sounds* – the album that inspired the Beatles to create *Sgt. Pepper.*

Left: The Beach Boys (l to r) Dennis Wilson, Al Jardine, Mike Love, Bruce Johnstone and Carl Wilson, with the Maharishi Mahesh Yogi.

Right: A shirtless and bejewelled Dr Timothy Leary. He preached the message of love – and LSD.

"I tried *Pet Sounds* as an answer to *Rubber Soul* and I understood that Paul McCartney really liked that sound," says Wilson, the genius who created America's "surf sound". "And then they went in the studio and did *Sgt. Pepper*! Damn!"

But what Wilson perhaps didn't realize when *Pet Sounds* was released in May 1966 was the impact it would have on the Beatles – and

McCartney in particular: "Without *Pet Sounds, Sgt. Pepper* wouldn't have happened ... *Pepper* was an attempt to equal *Pet Sounds*."

With *Pet Sounds*' complex arrangements, vocal harmonies and unusual sound effects ringing in his ears, McCartney led the Beatles into Abbey Road Studios to make what would turn out to be their most successful album.

However, in April 1966, a month before *Pet Sounds* was released, the Beatles set off in a new direction, one that would have a major impact on their recordings for years to come. 'Tomorrow Never Knows' had a working title of 'Mark 1' when it was recorded over two days (April 6 and 7) with producer George Martin at the controls.

The song was inspired by Lennon's increased use of LSD and being in what he described as his "*Tibetan Book of the Dead period*", after reading Dr Timothy Leary's book, *The Psychedelic Experience: A Manual Based on the Tibetan Book of the Dead*. Describing the track as "my first psychedelic song", Lennon explained that he wanted thousands of monks chanting in the background but realized that "it was impractical". Despite accusations that drugs played a major part in the Beatles' work around this time, McCartney accepts that while 'Tomorrow Never Knows' is an LSD song, it was "probably the only one".

The groundbreaking, experimental processes used in the studio involved Lennon's voice being put through a rotating Leslie speaker inside a Hammond organ, plus the use of tape loops to create strange sounds. At one point, according to Martin, there were "a total of eight machines in different control rooms throughout the building all linked up with people – including the Beatles – holding the tape tension by means of a pencil". Added into the mix was ADT (artificial double tracking), invented by Abbey Road technical manager Ken Townsend, which involved laying one sound on top of another and then moving them to create two sounds.

Townsend recalls, "As early as 1965, I tried double-tracking things with a single four-track machine and a single tape machine. John was always intrigued by the sounds you could create artificially. As a technical engineer, it was my job to translate what he wanted and work out a way to do it." And John's response to this new artificial way of creating double sounds was, "'We got ADT' – and that was beautiful."

Dubbed "Ken's Flanger" by Lennon, ADT first occurred when Townsend began to experiment with double tracking using a single four-track machine and single tape machine in an effort to improve the Beatles' working life. "Paul had been double-tracking his voice but it was not

> ## " We've had enough performing now. I can't imagine a reason which would make us do any sort of tour ever again. "
>
> *JOHN LENNON*

the easiest thing to do and John was spooling the tape echo machine back and he was intrigued by the sound of the machine going backwards. Some of those things were what led to 'Tomorrow Never Knows'."

The Beatles had fallen head-first down the rabbit hole of studio experimentation and, as the *Revolver* album debuted at the top of the charts, reviewers were forced to sit up and take notice. Acknowledging that the album had "new sounds and new ideas", *NME* analysed the fade-out track (the title emerging from a Ringo Starr-ism) and concluded, "Tomorrow Never Knows tells you to 'turn off your mind, relax and float downstream'. But how can you relax with the electronic, outer space noises, often sounding like seagulls!"

Three months before *Revolver* came out, *Pet Sounds* had arrived and, while it made little impact on the recording of the Beatles' seventh album, it eventually reached number two in the UK chart (behind *Revolver*) and inspired McCartney to aim even higher with his group's next release, *Sgt. Pepper*. However, according to a story doing the rounds at the time, that now-famous album title was not the first title they had in mind.

In the aftermath of their contract negotiations with EMI during the mid-sixties, which left the Beatles technically out of contract as they began work on their new album, an industry rumour revealed, perhaps

jokingly, that the Beatles were planning to call their next release *One Down, Six to Go*. It never happened. But McCartney did have an idea.

"*Sgt. Pepper* is Paul after a trip to America," Lennon joked. "The whole West Coast long-named group thing was coming in – Fred and His Incredible Shrinking Grateful Airplanes – he was influenced by that."

McCartney explained that the title came from him "just thinking nice words, like Sergeant Pepper and Lonely Hearts Club, and they came together for no reason." When he returned to London, McCartney took his idea to the other band members with the suggestion that they "get away from touring and into a more surreal thing", which would involve becoming an "alter-ego band". But why *Pepper*? There are two alternative suggestions as to where the word "Pepper" came from. Roadie Mal Evans believed McCartney took it from an in-flight salt-and-pepper sachet, while others suggest it came from the soft drink Dr Pepper.

Between their last show at Candlestick Park, San Francisco, August 1966, and early 1967, the four Beatles had completely abandoned their clean-cut mop-top image in favour of floral shirts, colourful trousers and assorted neckwear, including beads, cravats and kipper ties – a look that would go on to epitomize 1967's summer of love.

By the time they appeared in promotional films for the 'Strawberry Fields Forever' and

'Penny Lane' double-A side single – released in February 1967 – each of the band was also sporting new facial hair. John, Paul and Ringo adopted the drooping moustache made famous by Mexican revolutionary Emiliano Zapata, and George had grown a scruffy goatee – and was rarely seen without one for the remainder of the band's career. The Beatles were both sounding and looking different.

George Martin remembered: "Once the boys decided they would not perform anymore and wanted to just work in the studio, building up *Sgt. Pepper* became a bit like working on a Peter Sellers record because you were building a picture in sound." Describing all four band members as "eternally curious", Martin adds, "They wanted to find new ways of doing what they were doing, they always wanted to look beyond the horizon and not just at it."

However, one Beatle was less convinced about the whole *Sgt. Pepper* concept. "I felt we were just going in the studio to make the next record," said Harrison. "And Paul was going on about this idea for some fictitious band."

Tony Bramwell agrees with Harrison: "I don't think it was intended to go into the studio and experiment. It was just time for a new album – get twelve songs together and go into the studio for a few weeks and it's done." However, it wasn't that simple, as Bramwell observed: "They were in the studio and realized that they didn't have any finished songs. It was probably the first time

Left: The Beatles, snapped by fans – John Lennon (top left), Paul McCartney (top right), George Harrison (bottom left) and Ringo Starr – on their way to work in the studio at Abbey Road, 1966, during the making of *Sgt. Pepper's Lonely Hearts Club Band*.

they had written songs while in the studio."

After spending virtually two months separated from each other, the Beatles reassembled at Abbey Road Studios in late November to start work on a track that they thought would be part of their next album. Lennon's "Liverpool song", 'Strawberry Fields Forever', was finished a few days before Christmas. A few weeks later, just after the festive season, McCartney began work on his own composition about his former home city, called 'Penny Lane'.

By mid-January 1967, both tracks were complete and ready for the new album but instead both songs were handed over to EMI to be released as a double A-side single.

'SGT. PEPPER'S LONELY HEARTS CLUB BAND'

The album's opening track is the song that would identify the album for decades to come. It began to take shape at Abbey Road Studios on February 1, 1967, the Beatles' thirteenth day at the studio since the New Year. Nine takes of the rhythm track were done in Studio Two between 7pm and 2.30am the following day. McCartney's idea of the group as an "alter-ego" of the Beatles was coming to fruition. On February 2, the vocals were superimposed onto the previous day's tracks.

On March 3, after a month of working on other songs, four brass musicians arrived at Abbey Road Studios for a 7pm session on 'Sgt. Pepper', and James W. Buck, Neill Sanders, Tony

Randall and John Burden added their French horns into the mix under the direction of McCartney. "I wrote out phrases for them based on what Paul was humming to us and George Martin," explained Burden. Once the "outsiders" had gone, Harrison added his distorted lead guitar solo to the almost complete work.

Three days later, on March 6, the opening segment of the new album's opening track was added when a previous recording of an orchestra warming up was dropped onto the existing tape. After that, there was the small matter of adding effects – an audience clapping, murmuring and laughing. These came from the studio's collection of sound effects, which dated back to the mid-1950s, a time when Peter Sellers, Spike Milligan and Michael Bentine recorded in the studio.

'WITH A LITTLE HELP FROM MY FRIENDS'

The next track begins with the introduction of "Billy Shears". Written by Lennon and McCartney together, a rarity at this time, the song was created for the group's drummer. The singalong style of 'With A Little Help From My Friends' suited Starr, although he refused to sing one of the original lines, which read: "Would you throw ripe tomatoes at me". "I said, I'm not singing 'throw a damn tomato at me?'" Ringo explained.

With the line changed, the song – which began with the working title 'Bad Finger Boogie' – was completed in 11 takes, and recorded and mixed during the last three days of March 1967. When it was finished, it was segued to the opening track to maintain the notion of a continuous show with a sound effect of audience screaming taken from a recording of the Beatles playing at the Hollywood Bowl in August 1964.

While there was never any intention of releasing singles from *Sgt. Pepper*, the song was quickly covered by two British artists. While Joe Cocker's version reached No.1 in the UK in 1968, Joe Brown's efforts a year earlier peaked at No.32 with *NME* writing, "It's right up Brown's street. It's an exceptionally good number." Brown was less convinced: "It was the first time I had done a cover. They did the songs so well, all you could do was record them and get them out before the Beatles."

'LUCY IN THE SKY WITH DIAMONDS'

The most controversial song on *Sgt. Pepper* is inspired by Lennon and McCartney's shared love of Lewis Carroll's *Alice in Wonderland* stories. "In our minds it was an Alice thing, which both of us loved," says McCartney of 'Lucy In The Sky With Diamonds'.

The general consensus at the time of the album's release was that the song is about drugs, due to the initials "LSD" being so prominent. However, both Lennon and his son, Julian, have always maintained that the song's title relates to a four-year-old Julian, bringing home a painting from nursery school, depicting a fellow pupil, Lucy O'Donnell, which he called "Lucy – in the sky with diamonds".

Rehearsals on the song began on February 28, although the Beatles used the entire eight-hour session simply working through the track. Recording was completed on March 1–2, when a Hammond organ and tambura were added to the rhythm track, followed by Lennon's double-tracked vocal.

On November 28, 1974, John Lennon joined Elton John onstage at New York's Madison Square Garden for what would be his last ever concert performance, and they performed 'Lucy In The Sky With Diamonds'. Earlier in the same year, they recorded the song together and released it as a single by Elton. It topped the US chart in January 1975 and Lennon was later credited on the sleeve as "Dr Winston O'Boogie".

'GETTING BETTER'

Recording the fourth track on *Sgt. Pepper* began on March 9, and finished three late-night, eight-hour sessions later, with the vocals completed on March 23. 'Getting Better', a song started by Paul and based on the phrase "It's getting better" – which was used by stand-in drummer Jimmy Nicol when he performed with the band in 1964 – and finished with Lennon's help. Lennon later claimed it was simply "a nice song". Over the past half-century, it has been recorded by multiple artists, including the Flaming Lips, Status Quo, Gomez and Cheap Trick.

In the midst of this recording, a new up-and-coming EMI band were ushered into the studio to meet the Beatles. Norman Smith, who had engineered the Beatles' first sessions in 1962, had been promoted and was now in charge of producing Pink Floyd. On March 21, at around 11pm, Smith introduced Roger Waters, Syd Barrett, Rick Wright and Nick Mason to the Beatles. "They were working on *Sgt. Pepper* down the hall and that was a big deal," says Mason. "We were invited in to see them – go and meet God ... or Gods."

'FIXING A HOLE'

For the recording of 'Fixing A Hole', the Beatles stepped outside Abbey Road Studios for the first time to record a session for EMI. On February 9, they went to Regent Sound Studios, just off Tottenham Court Road, to record three takes of the song.

While no longer an EMI employee, Martin was still allowed to record the band wherever he wanted, but none of the usual staff engineers were allowed on the session. He recalled that the new location was "a pretty awful little studio, very cramped and boxy". McCartney's song was finished at Abbey Road Studios in a five-hour session on the evening of February 21.

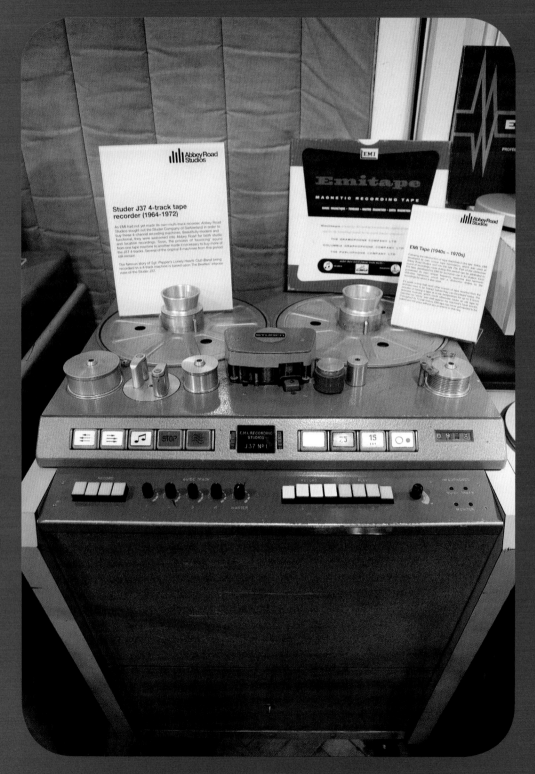

'SHE'S LEAVING HOME'

It was unheard of for the Beatles to record a track without one of them actually playing on it, but track number six, 'She's Leaving Home', is one of those rarities. On March 17, violins, violas, cellos, double bass and harp were recorded in six takes, playing a score arranged by Mike Leander but conducted by George Martin. Three days later, McCartney recorded his lead vocal, alongside Lennon's backing vocals.

McCartney was inspired to write the song by a newspaper article he read a month earlier, about a 17-year-old schoolgirl who ran away from her London home. The girl in question was Melanie Coe. Three years earlier, on October 4, 1963, Coe had won a dancing contest on the television music programme *Ready Steady Go!* and had been presented with her prize by McCartney, when the Beatles made their debut on the show.

'BEING FOR THE BENEFIT OF MR. KITE'

The song takes its title from an 1843 circus poster found by Lennon in an antique shop in Sevenoaks, when the Beatles were filming a promotional film in Kent in January 1967. The poster boasted the line "Last Night But Three!" before running into the words "Being For The Benefit Of Mr Kite". The poster continued with a list of famous performers in Pablo Fanque's Circus Royal, including the titular William Kite and John Henderson, "the celebrated Somerset thrower".

Recording began on February 17, with a basic rhythm track onto which was added the harmonium – played by Martin – before the song was given a unique background sound collage of Sousa marches to create the fairground effect. Martin, in fact, had chopped up tape reels of old Sousa recordings, thrown them up in the air and reassembled them in a random order. The producer said, "It really worked well. John was delighted with the result."

Three harmonicas – played by Harrison, plus Mal Evans and Neil Aspinall – Lennon's organ and McCartney's lead guitar were added on March 28, before sound effects and the final burst of organ and glockenspiel completed the song and side one of *Sgt. Pepper* on March 31.

" We got in a rut, going round the world. It was a different audience each day, but we were doing the same things. Nobody could hear. It was just a bloody big row "

GEORGE HARRISON

SGT. PEPPER: SIDE TWO

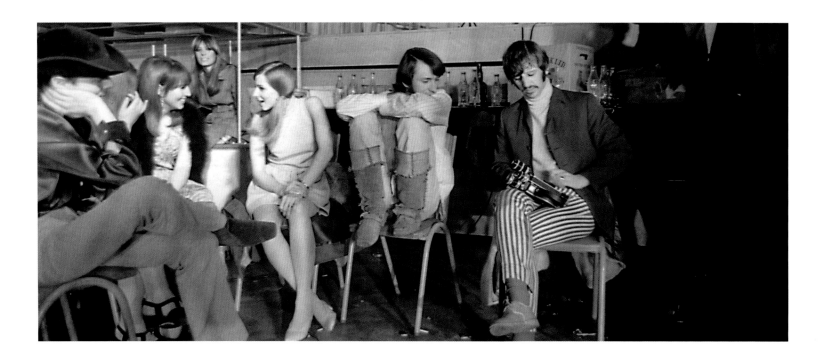

'WITHIN YOU WITHOUT YOU'

Side two of *Sgt. Pepper* opens with 'Within You Without You', the only track on the album written by George Harrison. The song began life without a title and no other Beatles were involved in the recording, which took place on March 15, 1967.

However, 'Within You Without You' wasn't the first song the guitarist suggested for inclusion on *Sgt. Pepper*. 'Only A Northern Song' began life as 'Not Known' when the Beatles worked on it over two days in February 1967. However, producer Martin was not impressed with Harrison's effort and decided to exclude

it from the final cut. "As far as *Pepper* was concerned I did not think his song would be good enough," Martin explained. "When he came up with 'Within You Without You' it was a bit of a relief. I still didn't think of it as a great song, but I found what George wanted to do with the song fascinating."

Influenced by Hindu teaching alongside verses from the New Testament gospels of Matthew and Mark, Harrison assembled a number of musicians from the Asian Music Circle in north London, while Neil Aspinall played the tambura. Although he wasn't involved in the recording, it seems that Lennon

was at Abbey Road Studios when the song was being recorded. "George has done a great Indian one," he said. "We came along one night and he had about 400 Indian fellas playing and it was a great swinging evening, as they say."

Another visitor to the studio that night was artist, and friend, Peter Blake, who would later play a major role in the look of *Sgt. Pepper*.

Above: In the studio, Monkee Mike Nesmith (second right) looks on while Ringo Starr plays.

Right: Paul McCartney conducts the 40-piece orchestra assembled for the recording of 'A Day In The Life' in February 1967.

"We went into one room," Lennon remembered, "and George was sitting on the floor playing with about 20 Indian musicians".

After adding more Indian instrumentation a week later, Harrison finished the song with an 11-hour session on April 3, when he added his sitar solo to the eight violins and three cellos, conducted by George Martin.

'WHEN I'M SIXTY-FOUR'

The track placed ninth in the album's running order was one of the first songs created for *Sgt. Pepper's Lonely Hearts Club Band* back in December 1966. 'When I'm Sixty-Four' is also one of the oldest songs in the group's songbook with McCartney claiming he wrote it on the family piano at 20 Forthlin Road in Liverpool, "when I was about 15".

Having been written around 1957 or 1958, the song featured in some of the group's live shows in 1962 but was not first recorded until December 6, 1967, when two takes were completed before McCartney added his vocals two days later. The final recordings were taped on December 20 and 21 when backing vocals, Starr's work on bells and three clarinets and a bass clarinet were added.

The song, which has the distinction of being covered by the likes of Alvin and the Chipmunks, Cliff Richard, Kenny Ball and his Jazzmen and Max Bygraves, was described by Martin as, "a send-up of the old stuff. It was also something to do with Paul's father's music as his father had been a musician in the 1920s."

'LOVELY RITA'

"Meter maid" – an American-ism for traffic wardens that McCartney had heard – was recorded for inclusion on the album on February 23, when the Beatles completed eight takes of instruments before recording McCartney's speeded-up vocal the next day.

In the studio for that evening's session was the studio's technical engineer Ken Townsend

but he had been out and about during the day. "I had been to Oxford to survey a venue for a session with Barbara Kelly and Bernard Braden and got pinched by a traffic warden. When I got to the studio later in the day, what did we record but 'Lovely Rita'. I mentioned it to the Beatles and they thought it was very funny."

The group recorded vocal harmonies on March 7, and the final burst of George Martin's piano was recorded, distorted via the tape machine, and added exactly two weeks later. For years, the Beatles had covered American R&B songs and 'Lovely Rita' marked the moment when the roles were reversed as the legendary

Fats Domino recorded his version in 1968.

It was now clear that McCartney was the dominant force behind *Sgt. Pepper* with more and more of his ideas coming to the fore during the making of the album. According to Tony Bramwell, Lennon and McCartney were visibly no longer combining to write music as much as they had done in the early years. "They weren't constantly in each other's faces," he recalled. They were also living in different parts of the south of England. "Paul was in London, but John was in Weybridge. He was too lazy to come into London unless someone was kicking him."

'GOOD MORNING GOOD MORNING'

The album's eleventh track sprang from Lennon's imagination after he saw a TV advertisement for Kellogg's Corn Flakes during days he spent lazing about at Kenwood, his Weybridge house. The advert gave him the idea for a title and a chorus for a song that would take two months to complete.

The Beatles began work on the song on February 8, completing eight takes between 7pm and 2am. A week later, more overdubs were recorded before brass musicians from Sounds Incorporated – who were managed by Brian Epstein – arrived a month later to add saxophones, trombones and a French horn. A selection of animal noises taken from the studio's sound effects archives were added in two sessions at the end of March to complete proceedings.

'SGT. PEPPER'S LONELY HEARTS CLUB (REPRISE)'

It was McCartney's idea to include a reprise of the title track just before the album's closing song. It took the band nine takes in a single session, on April 1. The song had to be completed on that day as it was the final session McCartney could record any vocals or instruments. He was scheduled to fly to the US on April 3, and EMI insisted on delivery of the master tape before then.

'A DAY IN THE LIFE'

Back in January 1967, the Beatles had started work on a track called 'In The Life Of ...', which was conceived by Lennon and augmented by McCartney in a true collaboration. It was renamed 'A Day In The Life'. Lennon explained where the idea for the song came from, claiming, "I was writing 'A Day In The Life' with the *Daily Mail* propped in front of me on the piano. I noticed two stories. One was about the Guinness heir who killed himself in a car. On the next page was a story about 4,000 potholes in the streets of Blackburn, Lancashire."

According to McCartney, the pair then wrote the song together. "John and I sat down and he had the opening verse and the tune. He got the idea of how it would continue from the *Daily Mail*. Then I threw in a little bit I played on the piano." In a *Rolling Stone* interview in 1981, Lennon described *Sgt. Pepper* as "a peak", and confirmed that the songwriting partnership was still intact. "Paul and I were definitely working together, especially on 'A Day in The Life', that was real..."

The next day, the two separate parts of the song – Lennon's beginning and end, plus McCartney's piano bridge – came together. But there was still something missing. On February 10, a 24-bar gap in the song was momentously filled by a 40-piece orchestra along with distinguished guests including Donovan, Mick Jagger, Keith Richards and Mike Nesmith

during a five-hour session. It transpires that McCartney wanted 90 musicians and EMI would only pay for 40 but by transferring the four takes onto a four-tape track he ultimately got the sound of 160 musicians.

The studio's technical engineer, Ken Townsend, was at the heart of the complex proceedings in the studio when 'A Day in The Life' was being recorded. "It was the only time George Martin ever got annoyed with me!" he recalled. "It got very complicated. We sent one take from one machine to record on a second four-track and then did another take and then got another set of takes and remixed using three machines. Although the machines were locked in, they didn't start together. It was a real problem."

Finally, on February 22, the final, crashing piano note that signalled the end of 'A Day In the Life' was recorded with Lennon, McCartney, Starr

and Mal Evans playing three separate pianos and hitting the same E-major chord at the same time. It took nine takes to get it right.

This was also the day when a young EMI management trainee encountered the Beatles. "After a session working with the Scaffold I went down to the canteen," recalls Tim Rice. "There was nobody there except the women behind the counter and suddenly all four Beatles walked in. I was speechless; there I was in the canteen on my own with the Beatles."

A year after the album's release, McCartney claimed that 'A Day In The Life' was a "turn-on song," and was written as a "deliberate provocation". He also explained that the high-frequency noise – 15 kilocycles, a frequency that only dogs can hear – was included as a "a bit of a laugh – 'Let's have a bit for Martha, Fluffy and Rover'".

After almost six months of work, the band had produced an unforgettable collection of songs that would never be performed before a live audience by them. For the four musicians who created it, *Sgt. Pepper* was something truly special. Lennon described the album as "one of the most important steps in our career", while Starr claimed that the album was "our greatest endeavour", and "captured the mood of that year", despite also admitting that it was the period when he learned to play chess, because he "had nothing else to do".

More than five months after the first track was recorded – and more than 700 hours of studio time at a cost of approx. £25,000 – *Sgt. Pepper* was officially released on Thursday, June 1, 1967. It was the first time a Beatles album was issued simultaneously worldwide with the same track listing and cover artwork.

Above: Beatles roadie Mal Evans with Paul McCartney (front), George Harrison, Patti Boyd and Neil Aspinall.

Following pages: Paul McCartney takes charge of the orchestra in Abbey Road's number one studio on February 10, 1967.

Right: George Harrison (left), John Lennon and assistant Neil Aspinall (right) on location during the filming of *Magical Mystery Tour*.

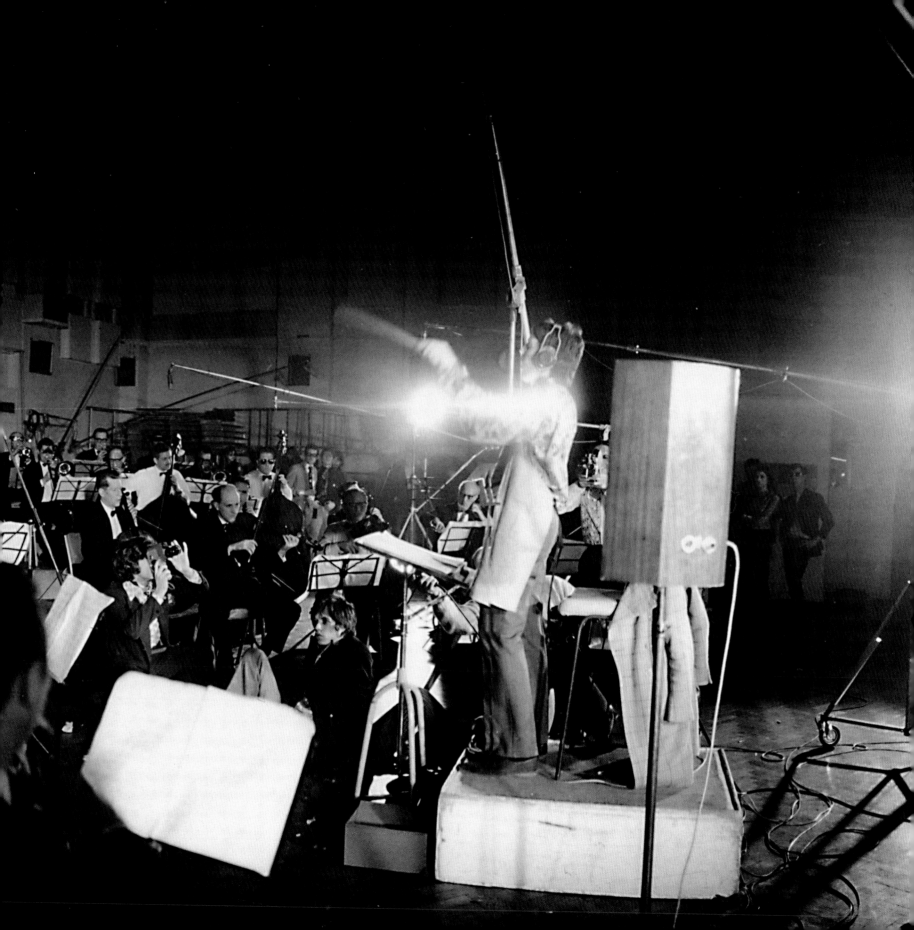

"We were fed up with being Beatles. We really hated that four little mop-top boys approach. We were not boys, we were men. We thought of ourselves as artists rather than just performers."

PAUL MCCARTNEY

MUSIC MEETS ART: THE COVER

Groundbreaking and visually stunning, *Sgt. Pepper's Lonely Hearts Club Band* blew the hinges off traditional album covers. In 1967, the era of powerful and striking visualization of music had arrived. For the first time, music could now be seen and heard.

With the concept of *Sgt. Pepper* "and the one and only Billy Shears" in the can, the idea now had to be represented in the album's artwork. When renowned artist Peter Blake and his wife, artist Jann Haworth, were introduced to the group by London gallery owner Robert Fraser, they explained their idea for the cover would be that the "new" band had just performed a concert in a park. It was then that Blake added the idea of a crowd standing behind them.

"This then developed in to the collage idea," explained Blake. "I asked them to make lists of people they'd most like to have in the audience at this imaginary concert." Haworth, an American who had moved to London in 1961 to study at the Courtauld Institute and University College of London's Slade School of Fine Art, remembers her reaction to being offered the job. "I wasn't particularly a fan of the Beatles but Peter was. We hadn't heard the music when we were offered the commission so it was a job

for something that we didn't yet know what we would be illustrating. I'm not playing it down. It is just that it was abstract and I wasn't in awe of the Beatles. We were asked to design something and we did."

According to Blake, both McCartney and Lennon made "long lists" of the famous faces they wanted to appear on the cover. Lennon's list included Jesus, Ghandi and Hitler, all of whom were cut from the final design, prompting McCartney to comment, "John wanted a couple of far-out ones, like Hitler and Jesus, which was John just wanting to be bold and brassy."

Meanwhile, Harrison's list, Blake recalled, was "all gurus" (four were in the final design), while Starr left it to the others to choose. With the concept for the sleeve firmly established, two issues remained to be settled: who would photograph the set that Blake and Haworth would design and would every living person chosen for the collage agree to be included?

Fraser's business partner was a photographer named Michael Cooper and he was quickly commissioned for the official shoot, while, at the same time, Beatles' manager Brian Epstein was given the task of getting permission from every living person to be included on the cover. These rights permissions were at the insistence of EMI chairman Sir Joseph Lockwood, who explained some of his concerns: "I said we couldn't agree to Ghandi because he was a holy man in India and we are important in India. Then I was worried about that little girl Shirley Temple because there were songs on the album about drugs."

Lockwood demanded that Epstein obtain permission in writing, or by telegram, from each of the celebrities. After a few weeks, Lockwood further insisted on "a several million-pound indemnity" from the Beatles to cover any legal action that might come from somebody included on the sleeve". Paul told me

> **" I asked them to make lists of people they'd most like to have in the audience at this imaginary concert. "**

PETER BLAKE

we wouldn't have a problem and that everybody would be delighted," concluded Lockwood.

And McCartney was almost right. The only official refusal the Beatles received was from legendary American film star Mae West, and she changed her mind after each of the group wrote a personal letter.

So, with at least some permissions and no blanket refusals, the Beatles joined Blake, Haworth and Cooper at the photographer's studio in Flood Street, Chelsea, for the capturing of the iconic album cover on March 30, 1967. A photo shoot planned for the previous day was cancelled because the Beatles were still recording. "We had everything set up with all the cut-out heroes and flowers," recalled Blake. "So the flowers went back and we started again the next day."

Dressed in outfits rented from theatrical costumiers Berman's – "we just ordered up the wildest things, based on old military uniforms," remembered Paul – the Beatles assembled at Chelsea Manor Studios in the late afternoon.

"It took about three hours in all, including the shots for the centrefold and the back cover," recalls Blake. "I think Robert Fraser was paid £1,500 by EMI and I got £200." Blake and Haworth, however, were further rewarded by collecting the 1967 Grammy Award for Best Album Cover, Graphic Design.

To create the sleeve, Haworth and Blake pasted life-size black-and-white photographs onto hardboard, which Haworth had hand-tinted. She had also made several cloth dolls, including her 'grandmother figure' and Shirley

Previous page: The complete works – the *Sgt. Pepper's Lonely Hearts Club Band* album and sleeve.

Left: Artist Peter Blake works on another project before starting work on the cover of *Sgt. Pepper*.

Right, above: The gnome featured on the album cover which – complete with the Beatles' autographs – sold in 2015 for £29,000.

Right, below: Gallery owner Robert Fraser, who played a major role in the creation of the album's sleeve.

Temple, who ended up wearing a sweater emblazoned with the message "Welcome The Rolling Stones", which was nothing to do with her. "It was just on her when I came in one day so I left it. Maybe it was Michael Cooper who did it as his son Adam was about that size".

While some of the characters were chosen by the Beatles, at least four others (actor W.C. Fields, singer Dion, sculptor H.C. Westermann and boxer Sonny Liston) were Blake's picks, while Haworth and Fraser also contributed characters. One of the people most notable by their absence from the sleeve was Elvis Presley, a man whose influence the Beatles had always acknowledged, and, according to McCartney it was because "Elvis was too important, too far above the rest even to mention – he was more than merely a pop singer, he was Elvis the King."

It took Blake and Haworth two weeks to complete the collage. "Peter and I decided who went where and then I nailed all the figures in position because Peter could not do carpentry," remembers Haworth.

The collection of 57 photographs – plus waxworks borrowed from Madame Tussauds' London exhibition of the four Beatles, Sonny Liston, Diana Dors, Lawrence of Arabia and George Bernard Shaw – were all tiered behind the "real" Beatles, who are standing in front of an ornate drum skin designed by fairground artist Joe Ephgrave. In the foreground of the cover, the word "Beatles" is spelled out in flowers – an idea Haworth picked up from a municipal flower clock in Hammersmith, West London.

While the front cover of *Sgt. Pepper* was a major talking point among fans trying to identify and explain the various figures, the whole album package took the significance of cover artwork to a whole new level. It was one of the first records to have a gatefold sleeve and include song lyrics, as well as including a set of cut-out items made from cardboard, including a moustache, picture card, stripes, badge and stand up – all designed by Blake and Haworth.

In fact Haworth was disappointed with the end product. "Our original thought was that the cover would be bright but the final look was too muted," she says, and photographer Gered Mankowitz was also less than impressed. "The concept for *Sgt. Pepper* was great, really impressive, but it was very crude technically, the photography was really awful and it was badly reproduced" he explains before adding, "This was a time when record companies printed their covers on the same cheap brown cardboard that was used for toilet rolls."

Freelance photographer Tony Timmington, who has worked for the BBC, *TV Times*, *Hello!* and *OK!*, is another professional who has reservations about the famous artwork. "As a picture the cover is not very good quality – it could have been shot on very fast film which is grainy," he adds but, as a 21-year-old living in Birmingham when it came out, he was more interested in the subject matter. "Back then we were just fascinated with all the people and who they were – and we had no idea who most of them were."

On the day *Sgt. Pepper* hit the shops, it was trumpeted as "the most expensive packaging of any British pop album ever". Over the years, reports have since put the final cost of the revolutionary sleeve at £3,000 – at a time when album cover designs rarely exceeded £100. As one of the most influential album covers of all time, it was worth every penny.

Right: Artist Jann Haworth created the cloth dolls which adorned the final sleeve design.

Opposite: Photographer Michael Cooper shot the Rolling Stones' album cover *Their Satanic Majesties Request* as well as *Sgt. Pepper*.

Overleaf: It may not be 1967, but the Beatles and *Sgt. Pepper* are still on show at a record stall in London's Carnaby Street.

"Sgt. Pepper is one
of the most important
steps in our career.
It had to be just right."

JOHN LENNON

RECEPTION

Ever since their 1963 debut offering, the release of a new Beatles album was always a major moment in popular music. Each collection delivered something innovative and exciting – even groundbreaking – but *Sgt. Pepper's Lonely Hearts Club Band* went further. It broke the rules, revolutionized recording and made headlines at the same time.

Despite the official release date for *Sgt. Pepper's Lonely Hearts Club Band* being set for Thursday, June 1, 1967, a number of people were given advance copies, or allowed to hear the album, before the rest of the world got their chance. It seems, perhaps appropriately given that the album was very much his brain-child, that McCartney was the chief culprit. When he left Abbey Road at 6am on Sunday, April 2, it is more than likely that McCartney had a selection of *Sgt. Pepper* recordings that he took with him when he flew to the US with Mal Evans on April 3. After landing in Los Angeles, McCartney and Evans flew directly to San Francisco in a private Learjet – hired from Frank Sinatra.

Following a tour of the city's sights, McCartney went to the famous Fillmore Auditorium, where Jefferson Airplane were rehearsing, and met singer Grace Slick and bass player Jack Casady. While McCartney claims, "I simply went there to see what the place was all about," Cassidy recalled more details, according to a report in *NME*. "McCartney brought a bunch of demos from the next Beatles album and played them to me. I couldn't believe they were that good."

While in the US, McCartney also flew to Denver to surprise his girlfriend, Jane Asher, who was celebrating her 21st birthday in the city while performing in Bristol's Old Vic touring version of *Romeo and Juliet*. This was also around the time when McCartney was a regular visitor to the Ashers' family home in Wimpole Street in central London, as Asher's mother had suggested he live in their top-floor flat as his London base.

McCartney shared the floor with Asher's brother Peter and he remembers McCartney bringing *Sgt. Pepper* to the house. "He was living in our house and brought round an early acetate and played it to the whole family." Asher was not only a prospective brother-in-law to McCartney (his engagement to Jane was announced in December 1967) but was also a successful pop singer with the duo Peter and Gordon. Peter and Gordon were often visitors at Abbey Road, during the recording of the album.

"I'd heard bits of it in the studio as it was in progress," Asher remembers, "but only odds and ends. But when he played the whole thing from beginning to end at home, I was astonished. And he left a copy at our house".

Above: Radio Caroline disc jockey Johnnie Walker on dry land for a change, circa 1967.

Right: The Beatles were on hand to launch *Sgt. Pepper* at manager Brian Epstein's London house on May 19, 1967.

Ahead of the official release of the album, the Beatles also took an acetate to the London apartment of singer Mama Cass, from the Mamas & the Papas. There, at 6am, they placed speakers in open windows and played the entire album at full volume so everybody in the area of King's Road, Chelsea, could hear. According to the group's former press officer, Derek Taylor, local residents opened their windows and doors and listened to the Beatles' new music without complaint.

However, Chelsea residents were not the only ones to get a loud blast of *Sgt. Pepper* in advance of its release. On May 12, before even EMI had begun to press copies of the album, pirate radio station, Radio London, moored off the coast of Essex, received an unforgettable exclusive and played the entire album, much to the disappointment of rival Radio Caroline DJ Johnnie Walker.

"There was intense rivalry between Caroline and London – we could see their ship a few hundred yards away and in fact we used to go over in the lifeboat and trade our Heineken beer for their Guinness," laughs Walker. "When we heard that London was going to broadcast *Sgt. Pepper* non-stop in its entirety, I realized we had missed a trick. I'm not sure how they got it but they were very proactive in their dealings with record labels".

Following the release of the album,

Walker did receive a copy of *Sgt. Pepper*. It didn't disappoint: "Everything about it, from the sleeve, the way they presented the record and how the songs flowed – it was staggering. It was like nothing else that had been released before".

Broadcaster Bob Harris also heard the new tunes when he attended a party at the Roundhouse, Chalk Farm, London, where celebrity DJ Jeff Dexter played an acetate of 'Fixing A Hole', 'Getting Better' and 'Lovely Rita', given to him by McCartney. "It was fabulous to sit and listen to those amazing songs," Harris said, "and exciting to think that we were the first people outside of the band to hear them."

In the final week leading up to the official release, Brian Epstein had advanced copies of the album, which he handed out to friends. Hollies singer Graham Nash was one of the lucky ones. "I became friendly with Brian Epstein. He gave me three gifts that rearranged my chromosomes: a 16mm movie of the Beatles at Shea Stadium and another they'd made to promote their single 'Strawberry Fields Forever'." The final offering was an advance copy of *Sgt. Pepper*. "From the opening notes, I knew it was an incredible piece of work," said Nash. "Listening to it there was wonderment. I played it repeatedly for days. I knew every note. I was stunned by the composition as a whole".

Tony Bramwell, Epstein's "second pair of hands", also gave away an advance copy to Chas Chandler, Jimi Hendrix's manager. Hendrix was set to play at Epstein's Saville Theatre on June 4, where Bramwell was also the general manager. "I gave a copy to Chas, who played it to Jimi at his flat in Montague Square, which was previously owned by Ringo Starr and would later become home to Lennon and Yoko Ono. I knew Jimi had heard it and thought he might do something at the show."

Bramwell's suspicions were proven correct when it came to the afternoon run-through. "Jimi rehearsed and painted his

guitar in rainbow colours backstage during the afternoon." As it got nearer to show time, the theatre filled with fans and artists such as Donovan, the Rolling Stones and the Beatles. Seated in a box, the group watched as Hendrix stepped through the curtain and walked across the stage playing 'Sgt. Pepper'.

McCartney was overwhelmed with what he saw and heard, exclaiming: "That was the

ultimate compliment. To think that the album had meant so much to him as to actually do it by Sunday night, three days after the release."

On Friday, May 19, Epstein held a small press party at his house in Chapel Street. Among the official photographers invited to the event was American Linda Eastman.

On the day of the launch party, *Daily Mail* columnist Virginia Ironside wrote an article

under the headline "What's happening to the Beatles?" where she proclaimed: "Since the early days of 1963, the Beatles have changed completely. They rose as heroes of a social revolution, everybody's next-door neighbours, the boys with whom everyone could identify."

She continued: "Now four years later they have isolated themselves, not only personally but musically. They've become contemplative,

---

Above and **Above Right:** The Beatles pose for the press at their *Sgt. Pepper's Lonely Hearts Club Band* album launch party.

After six months' work the group proudly displayed the finished article for all to admire. It wasn't long before the plaudits poured in.

secretive, exclusive and excluded, four mystics with moustaches and red spectacles, shrouded weirdos who nip off to India, and spend evenings at concerts of electronic music."

Just ahead of the release of *Sgt. Pepper*, the Beatles established a new business partnership, called Beatles & Co. Based at central London's Wigmore Street, the company boasted both Brian Epstein and his brother Clive as directors, although shares in the company were divided solely between the four Beatles.

In advance of the album's release, Epstein told the world's media, "I don't like to be particularly swanky about it. But it's going to be great." And, in general, the world's media agreed with him.

The Times theatre critic and renowned writer, Kenneth Tynan, wrote that the album was, "a decisive moment in the history of Western civilisation". *Time* magazine concluded that it was "a historic departure in the progress of music – any music". *Esquire*'s Jack Kroll simply called it "a masterpiece". Less enthusiastic was Richard Goldstein, who wrote in *The New York Times*, that *Sgt. Pepper* was "spoiled" and "reeking of special effects, dazzling but ultimately fraudulent". At the same time, *NME*'s US columnist, June Harris, wrote proclaiming "Beatlemania is with us again", as the radio stations in America that usually kept to a strict Top 40 singles format began to play the new Beatles album. American music trade magazine *Billboard* forecast that the "inventive album by the inventive Beatles should zoom to the top of the charts". Renowned US rock writer Greil Marcus, in *The History of Rock 'n' Roll*, announced, "No one had ever heard anything like it; no one has heard anything like it since."

Back in Britain, *NME* questioned whether it was worth all the time it had taken to produce but admitted that it was "a very good LP that will sell like hot cakes". *Melody Maker* journalist Chris Welch wrote, "The Beatles' new album is a remarkable and worthwhile contribution to music." In an interview with *Rolling Stone*'s London correspondent, Paul Gambaccini, in 1979, McCartney commented on the subject of the Beatles and bad reviews, saying, "I remember before *Sgt. Pepper*, we were coming in for a lot of flak. People were saying 'The Beatles are finished, they're rubbish.' Because we weren't doing anything, we were just hiding away in the studio out of our skulls making this album. And then it came out and they changed their tune and they said, 'They're alright, they're okay'." Within a week of its release, *Sgt. Pepper* had sold over 250,000 copies in the UK, debuting at the top of the British album chart, and ending *The Sound of Music*'s long reign. *Sgt. Pepper* remained at the top for 23 consecutive weeks. In America, where there were advance orders of over 1 million, *Sgt. Pepper* entered the *Billboard* Top 200 at number eight on June 24.

> ## " Everyone said, 'Ah! A concept album!' It was the first time I'd heard the word."
>
> **PAUL MCCARTNEY**

A week later it knocked the Monkees' album *Headquarters* off the top spot and remained there for a total of 15 weeks before being replaced by Bobbie Gentry's 'Ode To Billie Joe'. In just three months worldwide sales of *Sgt. Pepper* had passed the 2.5 million mark, well exceeding the sales of all previous Beatles albums. Bizarrely, the release of *Sgt. Pepper* didn't seem to warrant any US marketing campaigns. There were no advertisements for the Beatles' new album in any of America's three major music magazines – *Billboard*, *Cashbox* or *Record World*. In the summer of 1967, full-page adverts for UK acts such as Herman's Hermits, the Dave Clark Five, the Hollies, Manfred Mann, the Who and Peter and Gordon had appeared in most of the big US music papers. In contrast, Britain's music papers carried full-page advertisements to celebrate the release. They were both simple and effective and included a photograph of the cover's drum kit, a picture of the group, and one killer sentence:

Remember *Sgt. Pepper's Lonely Hearts Club Band* is The Beatles

However, in America, there was a dearth of advertising for *Sgt. Pepper* and, according to Dan Davis, it was all down to money. "When it came to *Sgt. Pepper* there was a great deal of 'why are we spending money on this band?' from within Capitol. I assume that they didn't believe in spending money on 'a fad' which sold anyway."

Paul Gambaccini, a student at the time, remembers vividly the immediate impact of *Sgt. Pepper*, "The student car park was at the opposite side of the Dartmouth College campus from my dorm. As I walked back that half-mile,

Sgt. Pepper was blaring from every dorm. I walked the entire width of the campus to the new Beatles album. The reception to *Sgt. Pepper* at Dartmouth was emblematic of the culture change in 1967." Gambaccini also noted that American writer Langdon Winner speculated that *Sgt. Pepper's* release was "the moment when Western civilization was most united since the Congress of Vienna – in 1815."

Immediately following release, *Sgt. Pepper* became much more than just another album: it offered a generation of teenagers a new identity. As with all great works of art, controversy followed closely behind. The BBC banned 'A Day In The Life' because they were concerned that lines such as "I'd love to turn you on" and "had a smoke" might encourage drug use. There was also concern that "4,000 holes in Blackburn" was a reference to holes in the arm of a heroin user. Lennon replied, "Hidden meanings. Everything depends on the way you read a thing. If they want to read drugs into our stuff, they will. But it's *them* that's reading that, *them*." McCartney's response was even more blunt: "We don't care if they ban our songs. It might help the LP".

Previous spread: On the eve of the *Our World* satellite broadcast of 'All You Need Is Love', the Beatles assembled inside and outside Abbey Road studios to promote the global television performance.

Left: Chas Chandler, who was given an advance copy of *Sgt. Pepper* and played it to Jimi Hendrix.

Right: John Lennon was unmoved by the controversy he helped create with 'A Day In The Life'.

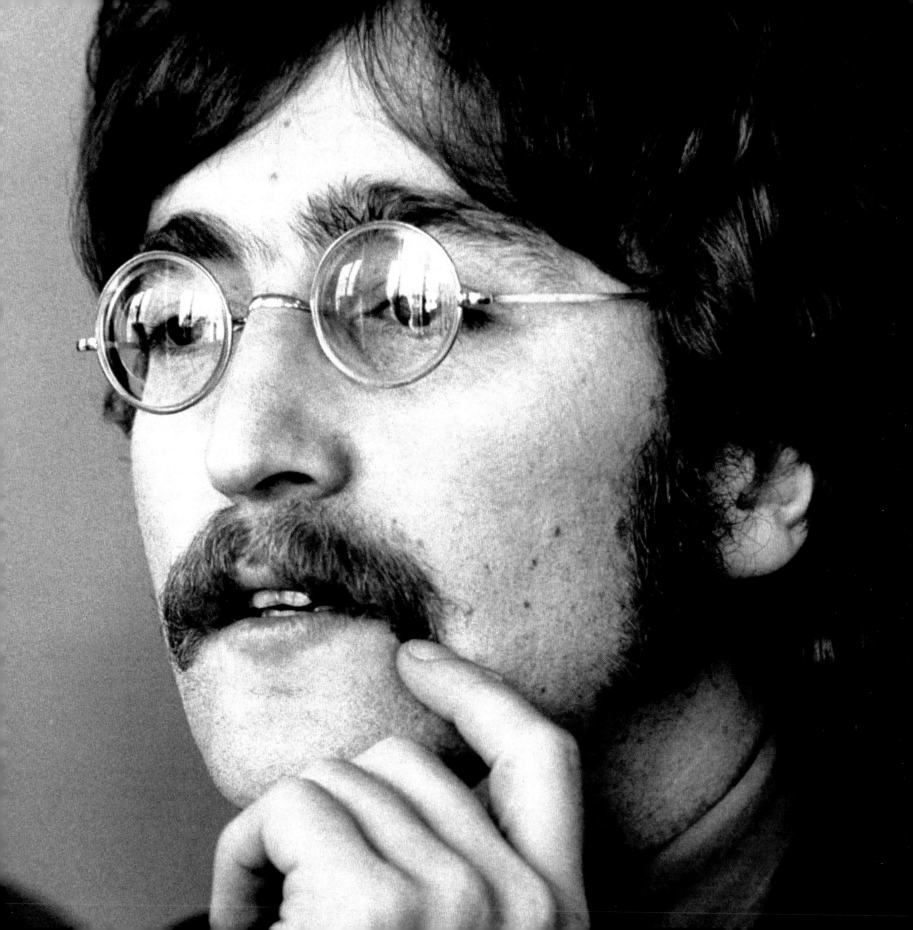

" Maybe we took ourselves too seriously.
A concept album is a joke to me. "

JOHN LENNON

Left: The Beatles in rehearsals for the broadcast of 'All You Need Is Love' with part of the orchestra ...

Above: ... George Harrison and Paul McCartney get to grips with some brassware, instruments they didn't usually play.

" God is in everything. God is in the space between us. God is in the table in front of you. For me it just happens that I realized all this through acid, but it could have been through anything else. "

PAUL MCCARTNEY

IT WAS FIFTY YEARS AGO TODAY...

Fifty years after its release, *Sgt. Pepper's Lonely Hearts Club Band* remains a crowning achievement in music. In *Rolling Stone*'s highly regarded list of the 500 greatest albums of all time, *Sgt. Pepper* took the top spot – ahead of the Beach Boys' *Pet Sounds* and the Beatles' *Revolver*.

In 2003, America's Library of Congress added the album to its prestigious National Recording Registry, honouring it as "culturally, historically and aesthetically significant". In 1977, at the inaugural British Record Industry Britannia Centenary Awards (now called the Brit Awards), a one-off event to celebrate both the Queen's Silver Jubilee and the 100th anniversary of recorded sound, *Sgt. Pepper* was voted the Best British Album.

In 1988, *The Guinness Rockopedia* noted that *Sgt. Pepper* "elevated the group to global figureheads for an emerging hippie counter-culture," while *The Penguin Encyclopedia of Popular Music* described the album as, "a carnival of pure entertainment". In the bestselling book, *1001 Albums You Must Hear Before You Die*, *Sgt. Pepper* is summed up poetically as "perfect pop in which ambition and melody twirl together forever".

But, with the passing of time, not every publication was overwhelmed by *Sgt. Pepper*. In 1974, *NME* – once the pinnacle of expert musical opinion and journalism – ranked the album number one in their list of 100 all-time best albums. By 1993, it had slipped to number 33. In 2003, it missed the top 100 altogether. In their commentary *NME* wrote, "Considered the ultimate achievement in recorded music at the time, the gleam has dulled on *Pepper*."

Reviews and sales figures often tell two different stories, but the official numbers for the Beatles and *Sgt. Pepper*, in particular, make for impressive reading. In 2012, the Beatles were calculated by the UK's Official Charts Company to be Britain's biggest-selling act of all time, with combined UK record sales of 22 million. The group's global album sales is estimated at a staggering 2.3 billion.

While Queen's *Greatest Hits* and Abba's *Gold* are listed as the bestselling albums in the UK, the Beatles and *Sgt. Pepper* take the title for top studio album, with sales of more than 5 million. Globally, the album's 13 million sales pale in comparison to the world's bestselling album – Michael Jackson's *Thriller*.

However, the impact *Sgt. Pepper* had on the lives of the people who were alive in 1967 remains fresh in their minds, more than half a century later.

Alan Parsons began his working life in 1966 as a 16-year-old apprentice at EMI's factory in Hayes, Middlesex. "I was working in a tape duplication plant making quarter-inch tapes of vinyl albums – this was in the days before tape cassettes – and I was in the fortunate position of being one of the first people to hear Beatles material that was coming out of Abbey Road Studios."

Parsons went on to engineer Pink Floyd's *Dark Side of the Moon*, produce No.1 records for Steve Harley and Cockney Rebel, and sell millions of albums with his own Alan Parsons Project. He explains the sonic impact those Beatles tapes had on him: "There was one that completely floored me – it was *Sgt .Pepper*. I had to find out more about how this was being done. I was, of course, a Beatles fan but *Sgt. Pepper* really did it for me. I immediately applied for a transfer to Abbey Road Studios, where I started as a tape librarian – just humping boxes of tapes around the place!"

For schoolboy Jonathan Morrish, Michael Jackson's former PR manager, one of the most intriguing aspects of *Sgt. Pepper* was that it followed the style of classical recordings – each track segueing into the next. "For teenagers at the time, this technique suggested it was as important as a classical record, this is a body of work."

Morrish, who went on to become an executive with CBS and Sony Music, also recalls a major moment at Clifton High School, Bristol, where he was a pupil. "It was a very musical school where we used to have a musical-appreciation class once a week. One of my abiding memories is that *Sgt. Pepper* was the first piece of popular music that made it into a musical-appreciation lesson."

As a 16-year-old growing up in Coventry, Linda Beechey left school and went to Henley College to learn shorthand and study English, where *Sgt. Pepper* took on new significance. "I never bought the album but our teacher used *Sgt. Pepper* as part of our English lesson," she recalls nearly 50 years on. "He wanted to know the meaning of it all and whether it was about drugs and, even though I never got offered any drugs, we decided it was probably all about drugs."

In 1967, 23-year-old Peter Asher and his singing partner, Gordon Waller, "gradually drifted into other things". While Waller wanted to pursue a solo career, Asher wanted to wander down a different path. "I wanted to be a record producer," he said. As the man who would go on to produce hit records for James Taylor, Linda Ronstadt and Bonnie Raitt, there was no better place to learn than Abbey Road Studios. "My ambition to become a producer was inspired by *Sgt. Pepper*. Every time you hear a really good record, as a producer, you wonder how they did that – that was the case with *Sgt. Pepper*. It was a period of great experimentation."

Renowned lyricist Sir Tim Rice was working at Abbey Road Studios when *Sgt. Pepper* came out. Fifty years on, Rice acknowledges the album's pros and cons. "It was enormously influential, but not always usefully, as it encouraged plenty of lesser talents to attempt over-ambitious projects."

Rice, the man who got his first production credit on the Scaffold's 1969 single 'Charity Bubbles', compares *Sgt. Pepper* with earlier Beatles albums. "I think in terms of sheer songs both *Rubber Soul* and *Revolver* were ahead of *Sgt. Pepper*, but I am really only comparing different levels of extraordinary brilliance."

For a Beatles-based radio programme I conceived several years ago, I discussed all the Beatles albums in fantastic detail with many prominent musicians and songwriters going on the record about their favourite Beatles records. For many, *Sgt. Pepper* reigned supreme.

Graham Gouldman, a founding member of 10cc, explained to me his thoughts on the seminal album. "The individual tracks on *Sgt. Pepper* work brilliantly, but as an album it works as an entity."

For Sex Pistol Glen Matlock, who received the album as a Christmas present, aged 11, in 1967, *Sgt. Pepper* is a mixed bag of ideas that "starts out as a concept thing and peters out a little bit. I liked *Sgt. Pepper* and a couple of other tracks. I suppose 'A Day In The Life' was a psychedelic moment at the time ... but I think it's a bit daft, to be honest!" Many people agree.

Over the years, many rock musicians have put pen to paper in order to tell their autobiography to the world. At some point, many of them have explained how they were influenced one way or another by the Beatles and focused on the individual albums or songs that influenced them the most.

Left: At the London Olympics in 2012 the Beatles and *Sgt. Pepper* were celebrated with a march past at the opening ceremony.

Page 81: The drum that was at the heart of the *Sgt. Pepper* sleeve was designed by fairground artist Joe Ephgrave.

Pete Townshend wrote in his autobiography, "For me, *Sgt. Pepper* and the Beach Boys' *Pet Sounds* redefined music in the twentieth-century: atmosphere, essence, shadow and romance were contained in ways that could be discovered again and again. No one believed the Beatles would ever top it or even bother to try."

Guitar legend Eric Clapton recalled hearing *Sgt. Pepper* for the first time at London's The Speakeasy when George Harrison arrived and delivered an acetate to the house DJ. "I was never overawed by the Beatles, but I was aware that this was a very special moment in time for anyone who was there." He also explained that this was the night when he first took LSD and was under its influence as he danced to 'Lucy In The Sky With Diamonds'. "I have to admit I was pretty moved by the whole thing."

Rolling Stone Keith Richards, however, was less than complimentary about the Beatles' seminal recording, calling it a "mishmash of rubbish". Richards also compared it somewhat unfavourably to his own band's 1967 effort, *Their Satanic Majesties Request*, claiming, "If you can make a load of shit, so can we."

During *When Pop Went Epic: The Crazy World of the Concept Album*, a 2016 TV show that aired on the BBC, narrator Rick Wakemen described *Sgt. Pepper* at the time of its release as the "most experimental record yet", which, he added, "expanded the notion of what an LP could be".

In its 50-year history, the album has garnered 17 platinum awards in Britain (each one awarded for 300,000 sales), collected a diamond award in America for sales that exceeded 10 million, as well as an unparalleled number of gold and platinum discs from almost every nation on earth. With music fans reminded in 2017 of the extraordinary music the Beatles created half a century ago, it will be interesting to see how many more sales the album notches up.

Right: In 2003 Jann Haworth created her own version of the *Sgt. Pepper* sleeve on a wall in Salt Lake City. Entitled *SLC Pepper*, it features the likes of Bob Marley, Jane Goodall, the Dali Lama, Erykah Badu and Tom Waits — people who, according to Haworth, "transcended celebrity, gender and ethnicity."

B-SIDE

TURN ON, TUNE IN AND DROP OUT

1966 IN REVIEW: THE YEAR THAT INFLUENCED 1967

In 1966, every teenager and twenty-something in Britain knew that they were living in the coolest country on the planet. At the heart of all the buzz, was the capital city that refused to go to bed. Even *Time* magazine agreed: "In this century, every decade has its city ... and for the sixties that city is London."

England's capital city had quickly established itself at the very centre of all that was hip and happening in the "Swingin' Sixties". It was home to the very best of British pop music. Groups and singers from all four corners of the land came, each with a dream to rule the world's pop charts, and all wanting to follow in the footsteps of the Beatles.

In his book *Ready Steady Go!: The Smashing Rise and Giddy Fall of Swinging London*, Shawn Levy confirms what anyone who grew up in the sixties already knew. "Nothing of the modern world we share could have been the way it is without those years in London. The music, the clothes, the hair, the sex, the drugs, the scandal, the merrymaking and the glee."

Right: The Beatles hold on to their awards at NME's 1966 Poll-Winners' concert.

Opposite: London schoolgirl Lesley Hornby went on to became "the face of 1966" – as Twiggy.

But not everything to do with 1966 related to music and fashion. The US began the year with their biggest offensive to date against the Vietcong in Vietnam and Labour Prime Minister Harold Wilson increased his majority in a March general election.

While the Beatles appeared onstage in the UK for the very last time in May 1966, Bob Dylan finally brought his new "electric" show to the UK and emotions ran high and cold during his performance at Manchester's Free Trade Hall, as the cry of "Judas" emerged from the crowd during his long-anticipated, non-acoustic show.

The summer of 1966 saw British music move irreversibly towards a heavier style of rock, which included Eric Clapton, Ginger Baker and Jack Bruce joining forces to create Cream – the first rock supergroup – and kick-start the "prog rock" movement.

Despite the arrival of a new breed of fashion photographers, such as David Bailey and Terence Donovan, and the launch of London schoolgirl Lesley Hornby as "Twiggy – the face of 1966", fashion was slowly moving away from fancy boutiques.

Meanwhile, at Wembley Stadium, England triumphed for the first (and, so far, only) time to win the FIFA World Cup, beating West Germany 4–2. At the same time, anti-Vietnam war protests were taking place outside the US Embassy at Grosvenor Square.

The Beach Boys, Lovin' Spoonful and the Mamas & the Papas forged a new path for American acts in Britain and, for the first time ever, the number of records by US acts in the British charts outnumbered those by UK acts. After a few years of dominance, attributed mainly to John, Paul, George, and Ringo, sales of UK acts in America also fell for the first time. For the British music press this meant only one thing, and, in August 1966, *NME* announced that the British beat boom was over. They softened the blow by adding, "Whatever happens, Britain has made her mark upon the world of pop."

While Chinese leader Mao Zedong was leading his country's cultural revolution and distributing copies of his *Quotations from Chairman Mao* (known in the West as the *Little Red Book*), Western intellectuals were out in force analysing psychedelia as the latest pop cultural phenomenon and what qualitative effect it might have around the world.

Hollies guitarist Graham Nash attended psychedelic sessions in America and reported that it was all about "trying to create an LSD session without the use of drugs". Meanwhile, *Melody Maker* published an article, entitled "Pot in Pop," in which a host of famous musicians, including Jimmy Page, Eric Burdon, Brian Auger and Spencer Davis, all denied ever smoking marijuana. At the same time, American drug and law-enforcement agencies were on the look-out for any references to drugs that might be hidden in pop songs, such as the Byrds' 'Eight Miles High' or the Association's 'Along Comes Mary'.

Following the murder in September of South African President Hendrik Verwoerd in the country's House of Assembly by a white extremist, 144 people died when a heap of coal waste collapsed on the small town of Aberfan in Wales and 100 people were killed in Italy as floods engulfed Florence.

In America, 1966 came to a close with four

actor-musicians who weren't allowed to play their instruments and who were created by a TV network topping the TV ratings and both the singles and album charts with their first releases – Monkee-mania had arrived!

In the UK, a different singing sensation with an axe to grind appeared in the form of a young guitarist named Jimi Hendrix. He released his first single, 'Hey Joe', and made his debut on British TV and drew complaints for his onstage antics from Mary Whitehouse, leader of the National Viewers' and Listeners' Association.

In December, in the face of a Musicians' Union ban on artists miming on TV shows, the groundbreaking show *Ready Steady Go!* went off air after three and a half years. The Beatles didn't finish the year obn a high note either, according to Tony Bramwell. "In August, they had released *Revolver* and then the disastrous 'Jesus' situation came to a head – stamp out the Beatles and all that nonsense – and then came their final ever gig at Candlestick Park. Nobody knew what was going to happen after that because they were all in a pretty bad state." With none of the songs from *Revolver* included on their final US tour, it was clear that the Beatles wanted to exile themselves in the relative sanctuary of the studio, where they could be free to experiment, to be themselves or, even, become another band. And, in 1967, experimentation was the name of the game for an array of new musicians from both the UK and the US. 1967 was the year *everything* got turned upside down...

Opposite: England football captain Bobby Moore holds aloft the World Cup following victory over West Germany at Wembley in July 1966.

Above: Paul McCartney and John Lennon on stage in Germany where they gave six shows over three nights in June 1966.

Left: George Harrison, Paul McCartney and John Lennon perform for the last time in the UK on the NME Poll-Winners' award show held at Wembley's Empire Pool.

Overleaf: Paul McCartney and John Lennon share a microphone on stage for the very last time during the final Beatles concert in San Francisco's Candlestick Park on August 29, 1966.

THE RISE OF PSYCHEDELIA

Looking back, it is interesting, fascinating and even ironic that the Beatles chose to play their last ever concert in San Francisco, the city that soon after would become home to a new, distinctive and – for some – worrying pop movement.

While nobody can pinpoint the actual day psychedelia emerged out of its chrysalis, there is no doubt that musicians, artists and their followers found their inner hippie on America's West Coast, in the City by the Bay.

Moving on from the Beat generation of the early sixties, the "flower power" and "love and peace" generation created their own community in the well-to-do Haight-Ashbury neighbourhood, contentedly called themselves "hippies" and worked towards a liberal counterculture with music at its heart. For the singer-songwriter Janis Joplin, the so-called "San Francisco music scene" was all about "the freedom to create". For other aspiring musos, it was creative licence to simply sing out of tune.

The psychedelic music that came out of San Francisco in 1966 – a year when radio-friendly FM album-orientated rock was already on air in the city – was focused more on pleasing concert-goers than record buyers and involved long, improvised jams often played by musicians under the influence of drugs.

The Grateful Dead, Janis Joplin and Big Brother and the Holding Company were at the forefront of psychedelic activities on America's West Coast, appearing multiple times at the Avalon Ballroom in the Polk Gulch district, alongside many other psychedelic bands. The Dead, as they were affectionately known, even took to living together in a small house (called the Dog House) at a commune in the city.

In October 1966, *Melody Maker* warned its readers about this psychedelic movement and the "freak brigade", citing the fact that only nine British groups were left in the *Billboard* Top 50 album chart. "With weird sounding names, strange looks and mysterious song titles, the Americans are first mopping up resistance at home. And there is a strong likelihood they will attempt a massive invasion."

A psychedelic invasion may have been on the horizon, but the "new style" American records released in late 1966 were greeted with a mix of caution and optimism. *Melody Maker* suggested that for the band Love, with their eponymous 1967 album, "It may take some time for them to gain acceptance but a lot of people will learn to love Love." The Byrds' album *Fifth Dimension* was deemed to be too "far out and weird. And a big seller". At the same time, more American groups were being formed, including the likes of Buffalo Springfield, Iron Butterfly and Moby Grape.

Britain had been warned, but, thanks to the likes of Pink Floyd, the Soft Machine, Cream, the Move and American "import" Jimi Hendrix, the seeds of psychedelia had been well and truly sown in London. The city's famous Roundhouse, in Chalk Farm, hosted a Pop/Op/Costume/Masque/Fantasy-Loon/Blowout/Drag/All Night Rave Ball in October 1966 with "strip, trip, happenings, movies" and free sugar cubes (minus LSD) for all in attendance – plus a prize for the shortest miniskirt. This was followed by the Psychedelia vs Ian Smith and the Double Giant Freak-out Ball – the former was on New Year's Eve 1966 and featured Pink Floyd, the Who and the Move on the bill.

Before the year's end, the most influential "underground" club on London's burgeoning scene opened on Tottenham Court Road. The UFO Club opened on Friday nights in a basement, which for the rest of the week operated as an Irish dancehall called The Blarney Club.

While London was awash with clubs and discos – Blaises, Tiles, Marquee Club, The Bag O'Nails and The Speakeasy Club, to name a few which featured a host of major pop acts – they did not fit into the psychedelic scene that was being played out at venues such as the Great Hall at Alexandra Palace where, for £1, fans could see Pink Floyd, the Move, the Animals and Brian Auger and the Trinity at events such as the 14 Hour Technicolor Dream in April 1967, and a Love In Festival, which partied from 9pm until 9am on July 29.

Melody Maker journalist Nick Jones, under the heading "An attempt at an explanation of psychedelic pop", suggested that, while the UK wasn't ready for "such a social revolution", there was a chance that psychedelia could "do the pop scene some genuine good". To back up his opinion, Jones wrote that while the Mothers of Invention's *Freak Out!* album was "on the whole, a very funny album", it did all depend on "how broad-minded, tuned-in and far out you are".

In the midst of all this musical turmoil, singer-songwriter Cat Stevens told the media precisely what he thought about psychedelia. "I don't know what the hell it means. It's a sick scene." In response, the Electric Prunes offered up their single 'I Had Too Much to Dream Last Night', which, according to the *NME*, included "strange rasping noises and electronic effects".

Despite their being dubbed "one of the first psychedelic bands", the Electric Prunes' bass player Mark Tulin claimed he had no knowledge of this exotic, new music scene. "Keep in mind that psychedelic came later, we were just playing what felt right for us. We didn't say we're going to be psychedelic. We were trying to add different sounds and, if that's what somebody calls psychedelic, that's cool." The bizarre names of the groups coming out of America's West Coast played a part in Paul McCartney creating *Sgt. Pepper's Lonely Hearts Club Band* and Electric Prunes' lead singer James Lowe explains how his group got their name. "We changed it from Jim and the Lords and had a weekend to do so before we went into the studio. Somebody came up with the joke 'What's purple and goes buzz buzz?' and the answer is an electric prune. I said it would make a great name for a band and we put it on the list, but the producer hated it and said he couldn't go to a record company with that name." However, when the producer was at a session with the Rolling Stones he told them that he had a band who wanted to call themselves the Electric Prunes. "The Stones thought it was a great name," says Lowe. "And the record company loved it as well, so that was that."

Meanwhile at Abbey Road Studios, there was a blissful ignorance of psychedelia and musicians taking drugs while recording. "Because none of us took drugs we didn't know what drugs were or what they looked like," says Ken Townsend.

While Townsend was aware that Beatles' roadie Mal Evans lit joss-sticks in the studio before each session – "it might have been to mask the smell of marijuana" – he says that it wasn't until 1970 that a sign went up in the studio warning musicians about drug use. Hollies lead singer Allan Clarke was also less than impressed with the new hippie movement and openly criticized bandmate Graham Nash in March 1967 when he told *NME*, "Graham talks a lot about the inner mind and psychedelic things but, to tell you the truth, I don't understand half of what he's on about. It's just weird."

Nash, a founding member of the Manchester group, admitted that he was the only one of the band experimenting with drugs at that time. "It was obvious the effect it was having on the band," he said. "Their perceptions about life were different to mine and the more beer they drank – and the more dope I smoked – the wider the division between us grew."

Around this time, Pink Floyd's Nick Mason elucidated his band's position: "We don't call ourselves a psychedelic group or say that we played psychedelic pop music. It's just that people associate us with this and we get employed all the time at the various freak-outs and happenings in London."

Following the success of San Francisco's "Human Be-In" festival on January 14, the West Coast's psychedelic influence had visibly spread across the country when, in the spring of 1967, 10,000 people assembled in New York's Central Park to celebrate the second "Human Be-In", an event that celebrated the key aspects of 1960s counterculture. At the same time, in London,

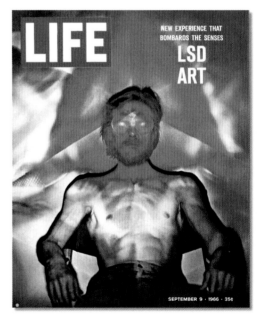

Previous spread: A couple share a trip on a rotating couch at a US psychedelic event where they looked at gods, demons and humans on a hand-dyed "cave wall".

Top: Graham Nash's enthusiasm for psychedelia led him to quit the Hollies.

Above: *Life* magazine from September 1966 showing a "way-out" cover photograph and in-depth look at LSD Art.

music journalist Chris Welch wrote in *Melody Maker* about his visit to the UFO Club when he witnessed "happening young people waving sticks of burning incense … with bells jingling, neck scarves flitting and strange hats abounding." He added: "Nobody can say psychedelic groups are monotonous or unadorned. They represent a colourful kaleidoscope of people, at present rooted in London, but which will dramatically alter the pattern of club representation all over the country."

However, there were those who were less than impressed with the capital city's music scene. "Hippies, love and peace, summer of love were just weirdness to me," said Chris Roberts. "As 14-year-olds we thought of ourselves as macho boys who played football. Flowers and stuff weren't for us." Dave Monk was also 14 years old and equally unimpressed by what was going on miles away in California. "I was aware of the hippie thing – it was all over the media – but only because of pop. Stuff like Jefferson Airplane, Moby Grape and the Electric Prunes were beyond me back then.

Despite living in the heart of Swinging London and working with the Beatles, Jann Haworth managed to avoid the impact of psychedelia. "It didn't impact on me at all. I was aware that people were smoking pot and didn't know they were into 'serious drugs'. And I don't know, did it produce better or worse art – better or worse lives?"

In August 1967 George Harrison, with his then-wife Patti and Neil Aspinall, travelled to the US and went to visit the vibes of the hippie hang-out at Haight-Ashbury. Speaking to *Melody Maker*, Harrison said that they parked their limo a block away to appear "the same" and then "walked along the street for about 100 yards – half like a tourist, half like a hippie". He explained that he had gone to find some sort of enlightenment but only found dropouts who had taken too many drugs. "Their brains were strangled. I gave up drugs after I saw that."

Jefferson Airplane, who conjured their name

out of a parody of the Texan blues singer Blind Lemon Jefferson, were on the bill when the Fillmore Auditorium threw a San Francisco Mime Troupe Benefit on December 10, 1965, with the Warlocks, later the Grateful Dead. The band are considered pioneers of the city's burgeoning psychedelic scene. Vocalist Marty Balin recalls that time: "Suddenly there was a scene. It was pretty and beautiful for a year or two." Following the arrival of singer Grace Slick, Jefferson's second album *Surrealistic Pillow* hit the US top three while the single 'White Rabbit' – a psychedelic take on *Alice In Wonderland* and *Through the Looking Glass* – was a US top ten hit. Balin suggested that the reason for its success was that "it was timely, for the era. The myth, the idea, the acid." Fans in Britain were denied a chance to hear the song as the album was released without the hit single and another track, 'Plastic Fantastic Lover'.

One man who remembers promoting Jefferson is Johnnie Walker, a DJ on the pirate radio station, Radio Caroline, in the summer of 1967. "Psychedelic music was America's answer to the Beatles and there was enormous competition between US and UK acts. I played Love and 'White Rabbit' a lot."

But there were those in the UK who remained unconvinced. "I was actually pretty contemptuous of the West Coast rock 'n' roll scene," explained Eric Clapton. "At the time, I just didn't understand what they were doing and thought it sounded pretty second rate. I thought most of the so-called psychedelic stuff that people were talking about was pretty dull."

Songwriter Tim Rice didn't quite understand psychedelia either. "It never quite hit me at the time," he said. "Maybe I was hankering after well-constructed songs. I might even have been a tiny bit too old for it."

For up-and-coming producer Chris Thomas, American psychedelic music was something he read about in the music press or talked about with musicians, but there was a growing UK

scene he could observe first-hand. "I saw Floyd and Procol Harum when I went to the UFO Club for the first time. Pink Floyd were basically the house band there."

Thomas also recalled that the newest music phenomenon was still only really happening in the capital city. "London in 1967 was incredible, the whole thing about the underground music scene was that it was very small. Like a secret. There was also a growing drug scene. Marijuana became almost ordinary. It just went hand in hand with music and then came LSD. Most of the people who wrote songs back then were hugely affected by marijuana and acid."

Iconic sixties rock photographer, Gered Mankowitz, admits that he and those at the heart of the music, art and fashion scenes in London in 1967 were "up our own arses having such a great time that we were insulated from the outside world".

Outside London, hippie culture still had a way to go to make an impact, although the movement did eventually head north with Midlands teenager Beechey admitting, "I had a bell round my neck and painted a flower on my cheek but we didn't have any real hippies, we just read about it in the newspapers and saw bands on *Top of the Pops*".

However, Brighton, was becoming a bit of "a haven for hippies in 1967", according to Peter Robinson, a former reporter for the local newspaper, the *Brighton Argus*. He also remembers the story of a local band called Span. "They went psychedelic and changed their name to Leviathan and signed to Elektra Records. John Peel was a big supporter." Their manager, Mike Clayton, was also involved in another aspect of Brighton's music scene. "Mike had a shop, which had a lot to do with making American West Coast-type music available – Spirit, Love, the Dead. It was the first shop of its kind in Brighton, very colourful, and fitted in with the 1967 summer of love theme."

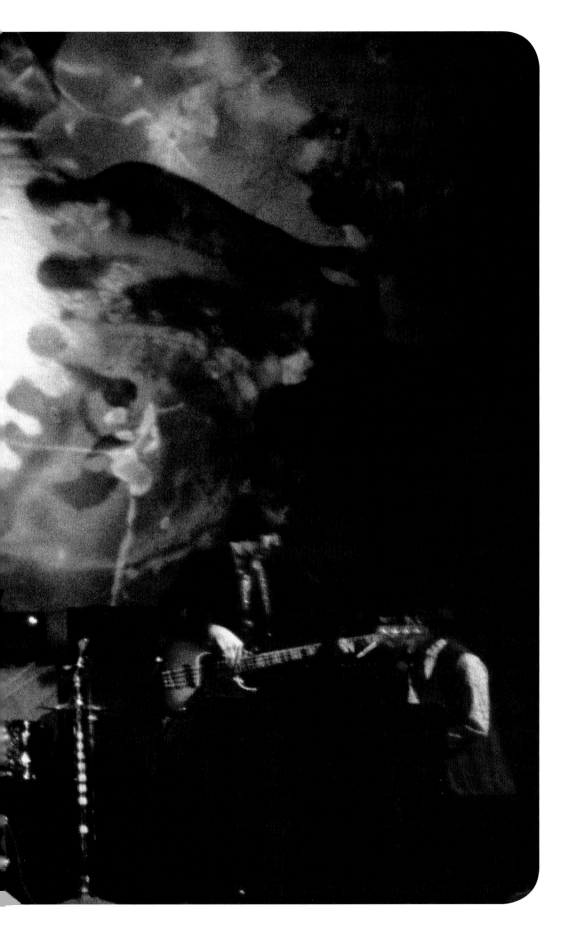

In 1967, *Billboard* described San Francisco as a "cauldron of creative activity" and predicted that 100,000 people would move to the city "to live among the hippies". In June 1967, the *Daily Mail*'s Anthony Carthew visited Haight-Ashbury and wrote, "Hippies call themselves the beautiful people and perhaps they are – to each other. To the outsider, who has not taken his daily LSD, they look a pretty sorry lot."

UFO Club co-founder Joe Boyd believed the club was losing supporters because of "a higher ratio of people masquerading as flower people", prompting Graham Nash to exclaim, "Flower Power is dead – killed by all the people who just weren't genuine. All the real flower people have moved out of Haight-Ashbury."

By the end of 1967, hippie-dom, and flower power were on their way to becoming a distant memory. *Melody Maker* reported about the "hideous commercialization of the hippie ideal" and the paper's major proponent of psychedelia, Nick Jones, was also forced to admit that, "one of the sincerest and major steps forward for the pop world has been systematically ruined."

To add insult to injury, on October 6, 1967 San Francisco locals organized "the death of a hippie", a mock funeral to mark what was seen as the crass commercialisation of the love and peace message and its generation of followers.

Left: Procol Harum topped the charts with 'A Whiter Shade Of Pale' and pioneered the use of psychedelic images during live concerts.

1967

THE YEAR THAT CHANGED EVERYTHING

Alongside exciting innovations in music and fashion – which introduced
the world to a host of new sounds and shapes – 1967 heralded a greater
awareness of politics and the power of protest. It all went hand in hand with a
youthful enthusiasm for happening, festivals, be-ins and love-ins .

JANUARY

Former Hollywood actor, and president of the Screen Actors Guild, Ronald Reagan entered mainstream politics when he was sworn in as the Republican Governor of California on January 2.

The first ever Super Bowl took place in Los Angeles on January 15, when the Green Bay Packers defeated Kansas City Chiefs 35–10. Over 60 million people watched the game on television and the winning Packers' players received a bonus of $15,000 each.

On the same night, the Rolling Stones appeared on *The Ed Sullivan Show* to promote 'Let's Spend the Night Together', but the TV network CBS was concerned with the song's lyric and the band were told to change the words.

A new rival to the Beatles, the Stones and a host of British bands appeared in the US in the form of the Doors, whose debut album reached No.2 in America in January and stayed on the chart for 121 weeks. Not content with upsetting American TV, the Rolling Stones upset British broadcasters when they refused to follow tradition and appear on the revolving stage at the end of *Sunday Night at the London Palladium* on January 22. Photographer Gered Mankowitz was a friend of the band: "It was extraordinary that they could do that and cause such a major sensation. They would always do the best show they could and then be in the headlines from doing something that was seen as a slap in the face for the establishment."

A book with a link to the Stones, Mikhail Bulgakov's *The Master And Margarita*, was published in Britain, 25 years after it was completed in Russian. The translation of the satire on Soviet society was given to Mick

Left: The continuing war in Vietnam brought protestors to the Washington Monument in America's capital city.

THE ROLLING STONES

The Rolling Stones' fifth British studio album, *Between the Buttons*, was released on January 20 and featured an album cover image taken by Gered Mankowitz at a time when things were changing in the world of album artwork. "The freedom and creative energy that had been released by the so-called 'Swingin' Sixties', coupled with an added confidence and a considerable improvement in technology, meant that I was beginning to experiment a little bit more freely," recalls the photographer.

The 12-inch-square format of the record sleeve was beginning to be seen as "a wonderful space to express something visually about the band and the music", said Mankowitz. His work on *Between the Buttons* was inspired by meetings with the band after all-night recording sessions. "The idea was led by seeing the band early in the morning when they tumbled out of the studio. We did it after an all-night session and drove up to Primrose Hill in London."

Once in position, Mankowitz improvised to get the desired shot. "I made a filter out of glass and cardboard and used Vaseline. I had 30 minutes with them before they got cold and really pissed off. The result was really successful and it was an album cover that was really well thought of even though the album was not their greatest."

With its soft focus, blurred front cover band portrait, and cartoons by drummer Charlie Watts on the back, it reached No.3 in the UK and No.2 in the US.

Jagger by Marianne Faithfull and the Rolling Stone has admitted that it was the inspiration for the 1968 song 'Sympathy For The Devil'.

The sixties space race was well under way by 1967, but America's programme was hit with tragedy on January 27 when astronauts Roger Chaffee, Virgil Grissom and Ed White died in a fire on Apollo I during a flight simulation at Cape Canaveral.

Under pressure from EMI for a new single, the Beatles reluctantly handed over the tracks 'Strawberry Fields Forever' and 'Penny Lane' in January and then assembled in Knole Park

Below: American astronauts (l to r) Gus Grissom, Ed White and Roger Chaffee on the launchpad at Cape Canaveral ten days before they were killed.

Opposite above: Action from the first ever Super Bowl match, between the Kansas City Chiefs (in white) and the victorious Green Bay Packers.

Opposite below: Jim Morrison (centre) led the Doors to their debut US chart success in January.

in Kent to make a promotional film for 'Strawberry Fields Forever'. A day later, pirate station Radio London gave 'Penny Lane' its first airing.

JANUARY NUMBER ONES

SINGLES

'Green, Green Grass of Home'
– Tom Jones (UK)
'I'm A Believer' – the Monkees (US)
'I'm A Believer' – the Monkees (UK)

ALBUMS

The Sound of Music (UK)
The Monkees – the Monkees (US)

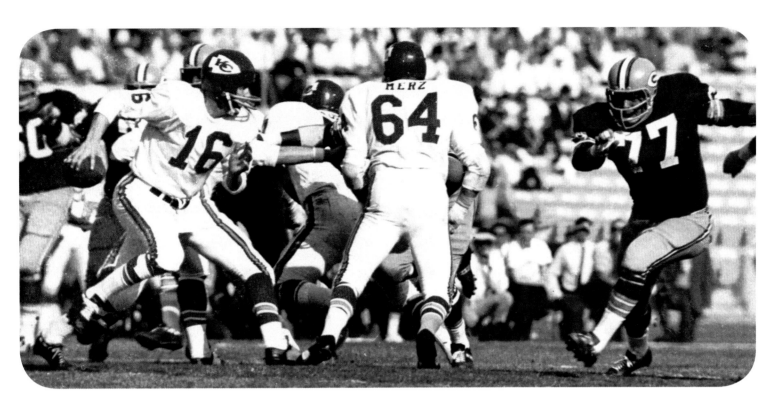

MONKEE-MANIA

By the end of 1966 the Monkees – Davy Jones, Mike Nesmith, Peter Tork and Micky Dolenz – were a multi-million-selling, chart-topping band in America with their own television show, but Monkee-mania did not hit Britain until January 1967.

The BBC aired their pilot show on the final day of 1966 and broadcast the first series from January 7 – scheduling it at 6.15pm after *Juke Box Jury* and *Doctor Who*. By the end of the month the single 'I'm A Believer' was a UK smash, with sales of over 750,000. Their debut album, *The Monkees*, soon followed the single to top of the international charts.

Reviewing an advance copy of their sophomore sounds, *Meet the Monkees*, *NME* defended the group's overnight success. "People are buying their records and watching their TV shows. They are not forced to do this – it's up to the mass to accept or reject what they are offered." As for the album, the *NME* declared: "This is good value for pop fans ... just enjoy the music, it's fun!"

According to David Roberts, the Monkees were incredibly important to him and his school friends. "We would talk about them at school after each show – the music was great, the songs were brilliant and they were valid." Over thirty years on Roberts looks back fondly at the four-piece group and admits, "None of us gave a second thought as to whether they played on their records or not or that they were 'created'. It was anarchic, it was stupid, it was American and, most importantly, your parents hated it."

Tim Rice, a pop music enthusiast, takes an equally relaxed approach. "They weren't musicians but actors playing a pop group in a TV show. It worked. It was fast-action stuff and there was a good song in each show. 'I'm A Believer' is one of the greatest songs of all time."

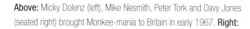
Above: Micky Dolenz (left), Mike Nesmith, Peter Tork and Davy Jones (seated right) brought Monkee-mania to Britain in early 1967. **Right:**

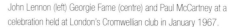
John Lennon (left) Georgie Fame (centre) and Paul McCartney at a celebration held at London's Cromwellian club in January 1967.

" Now that we only play in the studios, and not anywhere else, we have less of a clue what we're going to do "

GEORGE HARRISON

FEBRUARY

On February 3, pioneering record producer Joe Meek (the Tornadoes, John Leyton and the Honeycombs) committed suicide after murdering his landlady at his Holloway apartment. There were suggestions that he chose this particular day because it was the eighth anniversary of the death of one his musical heroes – Buddy Holly.

In the February 4 issue of *NME*, a review for the single 'For What's It Worth' from Buffalo Springfield opened with the quip "no relation to Dusty" before declaring that the song, "does not live up to their promise; uninspired and rather monotonous". Within months the song had become an anthem for America's disillusioned anti-war generation.

Two days later, EMI announced to the world that the Beatles had sold over 180 million records in the four and a half years since they signed their first contract with the company.

The world's first supergroup, Cream, were in trouble with US television stations over their promotional film for the single 'I Feel Free'. Broadcasters were concerned the sight of the three musicians running about in a wood and causing trouble in a playground dressed as

'STRAWBERRY FIELDS FOREVER' / 'PENNY LANE'

The record that has been ranked the "greatest pop single of all time" was released on February 17, 1967. Listed as a double A-side, 'Strawberry Fields'/'Penny Lane' – released in a limited-edition picture sleeve – were both recorded between November 1966 and January 1967.

After lengthy recording sessions, Lennon had two versions of 'Strawberry Fields Forever' that he liked and asked producer George Martin, "Why don't you join the beginning of the first one to the end of the second one?" Despite the two versions being in different keys and tempos, on December 22, Martin and engineer Geoff Emerick worked to speed up a remix of one version and slow down a remix of the second in order to create the finished track.

Inspired by Lennon's song about Liverpool, McCartney came up with 'Penny Lane', a track about a bus depot where the two young friends would often meet, in a district of south Liverpool. "Those two songs were the lead single. They were the first things we tried in the batch of new recordings," recalled McCartney, who began recording the song on December 29, 1966, and completed it on January 17, 1967, the day trumpeter Dave Mason, from the New Philharmonic Orchestra, was recruited to add two piccolo trumpet solos. For these now-legendary solos, Mason received the standard Musicians' Union rate of £27 10s.

When EMI asked for a new single, the band offered these two songs, which were then instantly removed from the potential track listing of *Sgt. Pepper*. They became the Beatles first singles not to reach No.1 in the UK since 'Please Please Me'. The band's run of 11 consecutive UK No.1s was over, defeated by Engelbert Humperdinck's 'Release Me'. In the US, where the two songs were issued separately, 'Penny Lane' reached No.1 while 'Strawberry Fields Forever' peaked at No.8.

To promote the duelling singles, the Beatles starred in two promotional films and Tony Bramwell recalls working on the video concepts with Klaus Voormann, *Revolver*'s album designer and friend to the band since the Hamburg days. "Klaus doodled this giant harp, which he suggested we build and then revolve the film around the instrument to create a musical effect for 'Strawberry Fields Forever'. We had to come up with something that looked like a giant harp and a film researcher came up with this old oak tree in Knole Park, near Sevenoaks."

With Swedish director Peter Goldman on board, the Beatles' team of assistants obtained an old piano and decorated the tree with lights. The plan, according to Bramwell, was for fans to "think it was wonderful, but then wonder what it was all about". Part of the filming for the 'Penny Lane' film was also done in Knole Park, with other footage shot in Angel Lane near Stratford station in London's East End.

When the double-A-side single was released, *NME*'s Derek Johnson decided, "it was certainly the most unusual and way-out

single the Beatles have yet produced in lyrical content and scoring", adding, "Quite honestly, I don't really know what to make of it." While Peter Asher can't remember exactly when he first heard either of the songs, he does recall McCartney discussing the idea for 'Penny Lane'. "I do remember him talking about using the Bach trumpet stuff with my mother who was a musician."

Left: Poet Allen Ginsberg (left) leads the chanting at the Human Be-In held in San Francisco's Golden Gate Park in 1967. The event, which was also known as the "Gathering of the Tribes", was advertised around the city on flyers (inset, left).

monks might offend some viewers.

On February 12, Mick Jagger and Keith Richards were served with court summonses alleging offences under the Dangerous Drugs Act after 20 Sussex police officers raided Richards's Redlands home following a tip-off from the *News of the World*. "When we got busted it suddenly made us realize that this was a whole different ball game and that was when the fun stopped," Richards confirmed. "Up until then it has been as though London existed in a beautiful space where you could do anything you wanted."

A rival to the long-standing British satirical magazine *Private Eye* appeared on the newsstands in February when the UK version of *Oz* magazine was launched by Australians Richard Neville, Martin Sharp and Richard Walsh. The monthly "underground" magazine featured noted Australian writers Germaine Greer and Lillian Roxon and cost 2s. 6d.

On February 18, in the US, New Orleans District Attorney Jim Garrison told the world that he would solve the mystery over the 1963 assassination of President John F. Kennedy, adding that it was part of a conspiracy that had been hatched in New Orleans. A week later, the twenty-fifth Amendment to the US Constitution was introduced and stated that the Vice President would automatically be promoted to the top job if a President resigned, died or was removed from office.

Above: Keith Richards (left) and Mick Jagger deep in conversation after being "busted" by Sussex police.

Left: The first issue of the new British version of Australia's alternative *Oz* magazine.

Opposite: Jimi Hendrix sets his Stratocaster guitar on fire at the Monterrey Pop Festival in June 1967.

Overleaf: They may have been rivals in the pop charts but Micky Dolenz (left) and Paul McCartney still hung out together in early 1967.

MARCH

March commenced with the Beatles taking home three prizes from the ninth Grammy Awards. While Frank Sinatra bagged Record of the Year with 'Strangers In The Night', the former mop tops from Liverpool won Song of the Year ('Michelle'), Best Contemporary Rock 'n' Roll Solo Vocal ('Eleanor Rigby') and, with Klaus Vormann, Best Album Cover (*Revolver*).

On March 3, a new British band took to the stage at the Finsbury Park Astoria. The Jeff Beck Group, featuring Ronnie Wood and singer Rod Stewart, supported the Small Faces and Roy Orbison. However, it was not a triumphant night for the band. "It was pretty much your textbook example of a 24-carat disaster," remembers Stewart. *Melody Maker* reported afterwards that the band had "created a very poor impression".

In their March 4 issue *Melody Maker* lent an ear to Jimi Hendrix's latest single 'Purple Haze' and declared that it was "difficult to assess its commerciality". They concluded: "If there's any justice in the world, this will be a top ten hit."

Pink Floyd's debut single 'Arnold Layne' was also put under *Melody Maker*'s microscope and the paper's reviewer pronounced: "Pink Floyd represent a new form of music to the English pop scene, so let's hope the English are broadminded enough to accept it." Band member Nick Mason admitted that the group's image was a cause for concern with various people, including their record company EMI. "They had acquired a band with a 'psychedelic' tag and, although we could deny any knowledge of a drug connection, there was no doubt that the whole movement that had launched us could not be sworn to secrecy."

The Velvet Underground & Nico album, from the five-piece band consisting of John Cale, Lou Reed, Sterling Morrison and Maureen Tucker, plus German singer Nico, caused much outrage thanks to the album cover designed by pop-artist Andy Warhol, also the record's producer.

Featuring a "peel-able" banana on a white background along with the words "peel slowly and see", the cover was viewed by photographer Gered Mankowitz as "a great collaboration," between band and artist. "And, of course," he adds, "it had all the phallic implications and broke a few boundaries".

On March 21, in the US, a convict named Charles Manson was released from Terminal Island prison. Aged 33, Manson had spent 16 years in prison before he was given an early release. In 1969, Manson and his "Manson Family" murdered nine people in California.

Right: These new "hippy" wax models of the Beatles were updated by Madame Tussauds in 1967, while fellow Liverpudlian Ken Dodd (left) remained unchanged.

Below: Walker Brothers John Walker (left) and Gary Leeds invited Jimi Hendrix on to their UK tour.

HENDRIX ON FIRE

On the last day of March, a nationwide package tour kicked-off at London's Finsbury Park Astoria. The Headliners were the Walker Brothers with Cat Stevens and Engelbert Humperdinck as support acts, plus a new guitar sensation called Jimi Hendrix.

In an attempt to steal the show and make a few headlines along the way, Hendrix set fire to his guitar by dousing it in lighter fuel. Publicist Keith Altham came up with the idea – "We tried a couple of experimental runs in the dressing room; it worked, and Jimi later used it on stage" – and as a result of the publicity stunt the American guitarist ended up in hospital being treated for minor burns. He also got a paragraph on the front page of the *Daily Express,* which read, "Pop star Jimi Hendrix was burned on the hand last night when his electric guitar burst into flames at the Finsbury Park Astoria. The show continued after the blaze was put out." The *Daily Mail* carried a similar brief news story.

As a result of the incident Hendrix and his manager, Chas Chandler, were warned by promoter Tito Burns that they would never appear on his shows again if they "pulled another stunt like that", while the headliner of the show, John Walker, was less concerned. "I just said to his people that, if he's going to do that every night, just let us know because we need a fire marshal. That was our only reaction."

MARCH NUMBER ONES

SINGLES

'Release Me' – Engelbert Humperdinck (UK)

'Kind Of A Drag' – the Buckinghams (US)

'Ruby Tuesday' – the Rolling Stones (US)

'Love Is Here And Now You're Gone' – the Supremes (US)

'Penny Lane' – the Beatles (US)

'Happy Together' – the Turtles (US)

ALBUMS

The Monkees – the Monkees (UK)

The Sound of Music (UK)

More of the Monkees – the Monkees (US)

Opposite: The oil tanker *Torrey Canyon* after it ran aground off the Cornish coast in March 1967, spilling over 119,000 tonnes of crude oil into the English Channel.

Right: Engelbert Humperdinck was touring with Jimi Hendrix when he kept the Beatles off the top of the charts in March 1967.

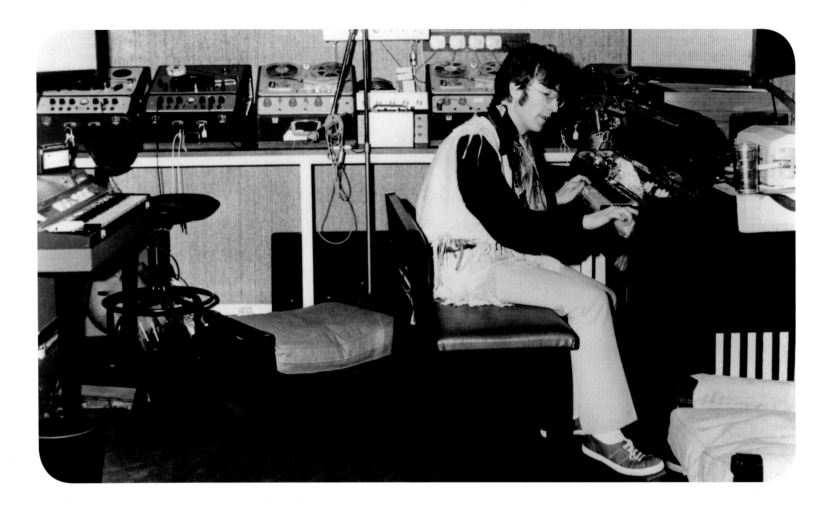

APRIL

The month began with Pink Floyd at the centre of a storm over the lyric to their single 'Arnold Layne', which no doubt helped it climb the British chart. It peaked at No. 20, despite being banned by the pirate station Radio London, because of its "smutty" content, but not by the BBC. In an interview with *Melody Maker*, Syd Barrett explained, "'Arnold Layne' just happens to dig dressing up in women's clothing. A lot of people do – so let's face up to reality."

On April 8, Britain had its first ever victory in the Eurovision Song Contest, when singer Sandie Shaw's 'Puppet On A String' won in Vienna. Shaw received 47 votes – twice as many as second-placed Ireland's Sean Dunphy – as well as hitting the UK No.1 spot. The single would go on to sell more than 4 million copies worldwide.

One year after changing his name from Davy Jones to avoid confusion with the main

Monkee, David Bowie released his novelty single 'The Laughing Gnome' on April 14. *NME* describes the effort as "a novelty number chock-full of appeal".

The next day, Saturday, April 15, saw the England football team's run of 19 unbeaten games come to end – at the hands of Scotland. The "auld enemy" beat the reigning World Cup champions 3–2 at Wembley Stadium in front of 99,000 fans. While those two countries focused

Above: John Lennon at work in his home studio at his house in Weybridge, Surrey.

Right: Sandie Shaw and 'Puppet On A String' earned Britain its first ever Eurovision Song Contest victory.

on football, America turned its attention to
the persisting war in Vietnam, where it was
estimated more than 400,000 US servicemen
had been deployed. Two protests in New York
and San Francisco on April 15 saw a similar
number of people protesting peacefully out on
the streets.

London's club scene was under the
microscope in Britain's music press. *NME* wrote
about the delights of the Bag O'Nails Club in
Kingly Street, Soho: "It's one of the few places
where one can still see London at its grooviest."
However, also according to *NME*, The Speakeasy
Club just off Oxford Street was still the club of
choice for many, with its mirrored doors, coffin
cash-desk and an enormous portrait of Chicago
gangster Al Capone, painted by popular sixties
artist Barry Fantoni.

During this month, Gered Mankowitz
photographed American psychedelic group the
Electric Prunes during a visit to England. "It was

a really enjoyable session," said Mankowitz. "I wasn't aware of the band, but James Lowe from the group contacted me because of my work with the Stones. They were into image in a way that most English bands weren't and we came up with lots of crazy ideas." Described in *NME* as "one of America's prime exponents of freak-out", the Prunes' single 'Get Me To The World On Time' was considered a "real raver" by the music paper.

On April 29, psychedelia hit London in a big way when the 14 Hour Technicolor Dream happening took place in the cavernous Great Hall of Alexandra Palace, north London, featuring Pink Floyd, Soft Machine, Tomorrow and Alex Harvey. More than 7,000 people turned up to raise money for the cash-strapped *International Times* magazine. Those in attendance also became part of Britain's first "Human Be-In" gathering, as the event attempted to clarify the "hippie ideals" of the underground movement. The *Sunday Mirror* reviewed the whole thing as "rather like the last struggle of a doomed tribe trying to save itself from extinction". *Melody Maker* reported that it was simply "a nice happening", and "the beginning of a healthy attitude towards total freedom for the individual."

Singer-turned-producer, Peter Asher was among the crowd at Ally Pally and found it "fantastic". Even though he never dropped acid, Asher thought the "Dream" to be "a fun event, but it was something that obviously divided generations". Tony Bramwell recalls how the event was actually billed in the music press as "a giant benefit against the fuzz" as it was the police who were attempting to close down *International Times*. "Nobody expected thousands of hippies to trek there, but they did," says Bramwell. "There were jugglers and fire eaters and, in one corner, from a plastic igloo, Suzy Cream Cheese doled out yellow banana-skin joints, which were supposed to give you a blast, but, since they were just banana skins, probably didn't."

Bramwell also recalls another VIP to the "Dream" that night. "I saw John Lennon come in, wearing an Afghan embroidered skin coat, and looking very stoned. He said they'd been watching TV down in Weybridge when they saw the concert on TV. They jumped into the Rolls and drove on up to London."

As the month drew to a close, Russian cosmonaut Vladimir Komarov died when his space capsule crash-landed due to a parachute fault. Meanwhile, in Greece, the army seized power in a bloodless coup which ended with Prime Minister Pangagolis Kanellopoulos being arrested and a military government taking over.

Opposite, top left: American "freak-out" group the Electric Prunes came to London to be photographed.

Opposite top right and **below:** Enthusiastic Scottish soccer fans at Wembley. When Scotland defeated world champions England, fans took their celebrations on to the pitch.

Above: Fresh from visiting America Paul McCartney (left) and assistant Mal Evans returned to London Heathrow Airport in April 1967.

MAY

On May 5, the defining "flower-power anthem" was released. Scott McKenzie's version of 'San Francisco (Be Sure To Wear Flowers In Your Hair)', written by John Phillips, debuted at No.3 in the US *Billboard* chart, but topped the pops in Britain, Germany, Belgium and Denmark, eventually selling more than seven million copies. When McKenzie was profiled by *Time* magazine, he explained that he had a problem with being a "spokesman for a generation".

On the same day, the Kinks released their single 'Waterloo Sunset'. It was welcomed by *NME* as "a real corker", heaping praise on Ray Davies for his composing and producing talents.

Six years after President de Gaulle of France vetoed their original application to join the European Economic Community (EEC), the United Kingdom, together with Ireland, Denmark and Norway, were allowed to re-apply for membership on May 11.

Jimi Hendrix's debut album *Are You*

Experienced came out on May 12 and eventually rose to No.2 in the UK chart and peaked at No.5 in the US. In its review Melody Maker warned its readers, "Although it may sound very weird and freaky to some, you can be assured that this album is, repeat, is the real Jimi Hendrix Experience." The engineer on the album was Mike Ross-Taylor, who worked at the CBS Studios in London and remembers how Hendrix had a particular way of working. "He rehearsed for a while, plugged everything in and just played around on his own. I could not believe the sounds coming out of his amp. He started to play and it was just unbelievably loud – everything in the room was shaking."

On the same day, Michelangelo Antonioni's controversial film Blow-Up, starring David Hemmings, Jane Birkin and model Veruschka von Lehndorff, was awarded the Grand Prix Award at the Cannes Film Festival.

After their controversy with 'Arnold Layne',

Pink Floyd's second single, 'See Emily Play', released in May, was welcomed by the music press as a record that was "crammed with weird oscillations, reverberations, electronic vibrations and fuzzy rumblings". This was a time, according to Nick Mason, when the band were forced to play the Top Rank chain of ballrooms, where there was a dress code. "It required a jacket and tie, no long hair and no jeans. This not only meant we were prevented both from going to the bar for a drink and mingling with the natives, but also that our own small band of supporters would never have made it beyond the doorman."

The Who, on the other hand, had their own problems with their single 'Pictures Of Lily', which was banned by radio stations in May because of its association with the sticky subject of masturbation. Composer Pete Townshend admitted that it was "merely a ditty about masturbation and the importance of it to a young man", which he had been inspired to write by a black-and-white postcard of the actress Lily Langtry, a mistress of the man who would become King Edward VII.

On May 20, the FA Cup was won by Tottenham Hotspur, while the First Division title went to Manchester United, ahead of Nottingham Forest.

HAIL TO THE KING

May began with a wedding as "The King", Elvis Presley, married 23-year-old Priscilla Beaulieu at the Aladdin Hotel, Las Vegas. She was the step-daughter of a US Air Force officer and the couple met in Germany in 1959 during Presley's US Army service.

Since Presley's demobilization from the army in 1960, Beaulieu lived at the singer's Graceland mansion in Memphis – with his grandmother acting as chaperone – and on her eighteenth birthday she was given a scarlet Chevrolet and $3,000 worth of clothes by Presley.

The wedding service lasted just eight minutes and took place in the private suite of hotel owner Milton Prell in front of 100 guests with Presley's personal assistant Joe Esposito as best-man and Beaulieu's sister, Michelle, as maid of honour. After the reception the happy couple took Frank Sinatra's Learjet to Palm Springs to begin their honeymoon.

BLOW-UP

Ein Film von
MICHELANGELO
ANTONIONI

Ein Film von MICHELANGELO ANTONIONI mit VANESSA REDGRAVE, DAVID HEMMINGS, SARAH MILES,
JOHN CASTLE, JANE BIRKIN, GILLIAN HILLS, PETER BOWLES, VERUSCHKA VON LEHNDORFF
Kamera CARLO DI PALMA Schnitt FRANK CLARKE Originalmusik HERBIE HANCOCK
Produktion CARLO PONTI und PIERRE ROUVE im Verleih von NEUE VISIONEN FILMVERLEIH GMBH

On May 26, John Lennon took delivery of his re-sprayed Rolls-Royce. Two years after he bought a Phantom V, Lennon decided he was fed up with the standard Valentine Black colour and approached a coachworks company to re-paint it with a psychedelic design of flowers and scrolls, at a cost of £2,000.

On the same day, and in the light of the US Government's decision to increase bombing raids on Vietnam, 100,000 anti-war protesters took to the streets of New York. The growing anti-war movement was, according to Capitol Records' employee Dan Davis, a positive movement for his country's youth. "In the minds of many, the anti-Vietnam protest gave credibility to the young and made the tastes of the young far more credible. Hence the growth and, ultimately, the legitimacy of rock music." Paul Gambaccini, a student at Dartmouth College at the time, recounts how the war in southeast Asia affected people in America. "The Vietnam war touched all our souls. Remember, all American youth were subject to draft-by-lottery and faced being sent to this hated war."

Above: The German poster for the award-wining and hugly influential movie Blow-Up

Right: John Lennon paid thousands of pounds to change his black Rolls-Royce into a piece of psychedelic art.

MAY NUMBER ONES

SINGLES

'Puppet On A String' – Sandie Shaw (UK)
'Silence Is Golden' – the Tremeloes (UK)
'Somethin' Stupid' – Frank and
Nancy Sinatra (US)
'The Happening' – the Supremes (US)
'Groovin'' – the Rascals (US)

ALBUMS

The Sound of Music (UK)
More of the Monkees – the Monkees (UK)
More of the Monkees – the Monkees (US)

JUNE

Following the founding of the Vietnam Veterans Against the War Association on June 1, there were more anti-Vietnam-war protests, with 10,000 people marching for peace, and occupying Century Plaza, Los Angeles.

Less than a week later, Israel declared war in the Middle East and launched raids on Syria, Jordan, Iraq and Egypt before agreeing to a ceasefire on June 11 – bringing to an end the so-called Six Day War. Egypt then enforced a blockade of the Suez Canal and closed it to all shipping for the next eight years. In the midst of this turmoil, revered American writer and wit Dorothy Parker died.

Procol Harum's 'A Whiter Shade Of Pale' became Decca's fastest-selling single with sales of over 600,000. Taking advantage of the limited opportunities for TV exposure, Procol Harum appeared on the first edition of BBC One's *Billy Cotton's Music Hall* on June 17, alongside Roy Castle, Kathy Kay and the Tiller Girls.

Between June 16 and 18, the world's first major pop festival was held in Monterey, California. The Who, Jimi Hendrix and the Animals joined the Byrds, the Grateful Dead, Otis Redding, Jefferson Airplane and the Mamas & the Papas. More than 50,000 people turned up. The event was organized by the Monterey

Pop Foundation, whose board included John Phillips, Paul McCartney, Mick Jagger, Brian Wilson and Smokey Robinson.

According to future *Rolling Stone* publisher, Jann Wenner, reporting for *Melody Maker* at the time, the festival was "a superb moment for rock 'n' roll". *NME* proclaimed: "the entire event was a clear cut victory for the hippies." While Capitol Records' Dan Davis reported: "The festival made the nation as a whole aware that rock 'n' roll was for real." There was one act who weren't on the bill and Cream's Eric Clapton was not best pleased. "We felt disappointed that Stigwood [the band's manager] had not allowed us to play

the Monterey Pop Festival, especially having seen the incredible success that Hendrix and the Who had had there."

Over the same weekend, on the shores of Lake Geneva in Switzerland, the first-ever Montreux Jazz Festival took place in the Montreux Casino with Miles Davis, Bill Evans, Soft Machine, Nina Simone and Ella Fitzgerald on the bill.

On June 17, in the midst of all the rock and jazz, China became the first Asian nation to develop atomic weapons when it tested a 3.3-megaton H-bomb. However, there was relief for fans of the Monkees, when the US Army Draft Board confirmed that Englishman Davy Jones would not be drafted into the service.

When Van Morrison's 'Brown Eyed Girl' was refused airplay in America because of a line

about "making love in the green grass", the Belfast-born singer recorded a more acceptable version with the replacement line "laughing and running". The song went on to become his first solo hit in the US.

After *Time* magazine published an interview with Paul McCartney, in which he admitted taking LSD, the Beatle appeared on *Independent Television News* in Britain and told viewers,

---

Opposite: Israeli tanks advance along the Gaza Strip in June 1967 as what became known as the Six-Day War gets under way.

Above: Procol Harum on stage at the BBC during rehearsals for an appearance on *Top of the Pops*.

"I don't think my fans are going to take drugs just because I did." When *Melody Maker* followed up with a poll, the majority of the paper's readers believed LSD to be "evil" and stated that Paul was wrong to admit he had taken the drug.

On June 25, world heavyweight boxing champion Muhammad Ali, who had been indicted for refusing to be drafted into the US Army, and fight in Vietnam, was sentenced to five years in jail and fined $10,000. He famously said, "I ain't got no quarrel with those Vietcong." His jail sentence was quashed on appeal, but he was still stripped of his world boxing title and banned from fighting for three years.

On June 27, Enfield, north London, witnessed a historical first when actor Reg Varney, star

Left: George Harrison poses for a photo at the press call for the *Our World* television broadcast.

'ALL YOU NEED IS LOVE'

The Beatles' involvement in the first live worldwide satellite television broadcast had been announced to the public on May 22, but it was another three weeks before the group assembled in Olympic Sound Studios, west London, to begin work on the song 'All You Need Is Love'. This momentous day in history was June 14.

As representatives of the BBC and Britain in the programme *Our World*, the Beatles were given one brief: that the song should be simple so that viewers all around the world would understand it – and Lennon's song fitted the bill. Three more recording sessions took place in Abbey Road during the following week and on June 25, the group, a 13-piece orchestra and assorted guests assembled in Studio One at Abbey Road for the live broadcast, which was seen by more than 400 million people.

One of the guests at the studio was Graham Nash, who remembers getting an early-morning call from McCartney inviting him to the studio. "Everybody was dressed in their finest hippie outfits: Mick Jagger, Keith Richards, Eric Clapton, Keith Moon, Marianne Faithfull, Jane Asher, Pattie Harrison, and other friends, were there awaiting what was obviously going to be an incredible event."

Gary Leeds, from the Walker Brothers, was another of the guests. He recalls hearing the new Beatles song for the first time. "The Beatles did a run-through to check cameras and sound, which was the first time anyone present had heard the song. I loved it instantly, its structure was good and the message it conveyed appealed to me." Both Nash and Walker can be heard whistling during the end of the recording.

George Martin, conductor Mike Vickers (ex-Manfred Mann member), the orchestra and guests ran through more than 50 takes of 'All You Need Is Love' with number 58 being the live television broadcast. Martin had woven into the song's arrangement Bach's 'Brandenburg' concerto, the French national anthem 'La Marseillaise', 'Greensleeves' and Glenn Miller's 'In The Mood'. Martin thought all these pieces were out of copyright, but Millers's piece was not and EMI had to pay a substantial royalty to the music's publishers.

Melody Maker considered the song to be "a cool, calculated, contagious Beatles singalong" while *NME* declared, "it's very simple in construction so all the foreign countries could understand it", before adding, "One can almost hear the group's tongues firmly planted in their cheeks."

The version of 'All You Need Is Love' that was released as a single was not the version broadcast to the world, but nobody really cared, as the single became the Beatles' twelfth British No.1 and their fourteenth US chart topper. It was the first single to credit George Martin as producer.

of the TV series *On the Buses*, opened the country's first automated teller machine (ATM) at the local branch of Barclays Bank.

On June 30, following the police raid on Keith Richards's home in Sussex in February, Rolling Stones Jagger and Richards appeared in court, where Jagger was sentenced to three months' imprisonment for unlawfully possessing four Benzedrine tablets, and Richards was sentenced to a year in jail for allowing his house to be used for smoking cannabis. The two rock stars were sent to Brixton and Wormwood Scrubs prisons before being bailed.

Right: Boxer Muhammed Ali speaks to the media after his court hearing in Houston, Texas.

Below: All you needed to know about the Monterey Pop Festival was in this handy-sized hand-out.

Below right: British TV star Reg Varney gets some cash from Britain's first "cash machine".

Opposite: Two young fans take in the news about Brian Epstein's death while seated on the steps of his home in London's Belgravia.

Overleaf: Rehearsals for their global performance of 'All You Need Is Love' provide the Beatles with the chance to experiment in the studio as (l to r) Ringo Starr tries out the trumpet, George Harrison has a go on the flugelhorn, Paul McCartney gives the trombone a blow and John Lennon gets his hands on an accordion.

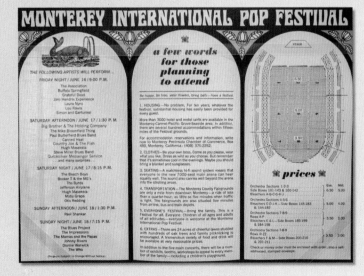

JULY

On July 1, reacting to the jail sentences passed on Jagger and Richards, *The Times* printed an article by editor William Rees-Mogg headlined, "Who breaks a butterfly on a wheel". It suggested that Jagger had received a more severe sentence than that given to "any purely anonymous young man". Other national newspapers followed suit and questioned the sentences: "Would Mick Jagger be in jail had he not been the lead singer of the Rolling Stones?" asked the *London Evening News*, while the *Sunday Express* declared Jagger's sentence to be "monstrously out of proportion to the offences he committed".

Gered Mankowitz, who began working with the Stones in 1965, was impressed with the stance taken by the press. "*The Times* coming out in favour of Mick was a big turning point back then. It became quite clear that when they arrested Mick and Keith and put them in jail, it was the establishment trying to draw a line."

The story rumbled on, and, on July 24, *The Times* printed a full-page advertisement advocating a reform of the cannabis laws. It was signed by author Graham Greene, artist David Hockney, jazz singer George Melly, critic Kenneth Tynan and all four Beatles, plus Brian Epstein. A week later Richards's conviction was

quashed and Jagger's sentence reduced to a conditional discharge.

Three days later, the British Parliament legalized sexual intercourse between consenting men over the age of 21. At the same time, the 70mph speed limit was made law after a trial period the previous year.

The start of the month also gave British television viewers their first chance to watch programmes in colour when BBC Two aired the Wimbledon tennis championships.

During July, America faced a series of race riots in several of its major cities. A total of 26 people were killed during rioting in Newark,

Left: Back from a group holiday in Greece, Paul McCartney and Jane Asher are left in charge of four-year-old Julian Lennon.

Right: Paul McCartney catches up with the news about the Rolling Stones on his return from Greece.

JULY NUMBER ONES

SINGLES

'A Whiter Shade Of Pale'
– Procol Harum (UK)

'All You Need Is Love' – the Beatles (UK)

'Windy' – the Association (US)

'Light My Fire' – the Doors (US)

ALBUMS

Sgt. Pepper's Lonely Hearts Club Band
– the Beatles (UK)

Sgt. Pepper's Lonely Hearts Club Band
– the Beatles (US)

and a further 43 people died over five days of race-related trouble in Detroit, while damage estimated at more than $4 million was done to property during riots in Minneapolis.

On July 24, during an official visit to Canada, to attend Expo 67, French President Charles de Gaulle made his "Vive le Quebec Libre" ("Long Live Free Quebec") speech in Montreal. It stirred up controversy among Canadians and French-Canadians, including Québécois, who were demanding sovereignty. The Canadian Prime Minister responded, saying, "Canadians do not need to be liberated."

A second hippie festival was held at Alexandra Palace on July 29, when Eric Burdon, the Animals and Arthur Brown played the Love-In Festival. It began at 9pm and ran through until 9am the next day. Tickets cost £1.

The Bee Gees released their debut studio album *Bee Gees 1st* – it became a top ten hit in the UK and US – and American group the Young Rascals issued their single 'Groovin', which topped the US chart and hit the British top ten despite its title being a euphemism for Sunday afternoon sex.

On an altogether weirder note, the Incredible String Band – the duo Mike Heron and Robin

Above: French President Charles de Gaulle gives his controversial address to the people on Montreal during his official trip to Canada.

Right: For just £1 fans got to see Arthur Brown (top) and the Animals at the all-night "Love In" at London's Alexandra Palace.

Williams – released their second album and decided to call it *The 5000 Spirits or the Layers of the Onion*. It earned the pair an appearance at the prestigious Newport Folk Festival in America. Paul McCartney also listed it as one of his favourite albums of the year.

Making less of an impression were the Grateful Dead, whose eponymous debut album – recorded in just three days – was described by a reviewer in *Melody Maker* as "mostly an ace drag, unless you happen to be stoned in your favourite club with your favourite person. Then you might be tempted to utter 'yeah'."

Left: John Lennon bought this gypsy caravan for his son Julian and had it hand-painted in a similar fashion as his Rolls-Royce.

Above: The pirate radio ship *Radio Caroline North* was moored in the North Sea, four miles off the Isle of Man from 1964.

Overleaf: The summer of love and Paul McCartney strums his guitar in the sunshine while John Lennon takes it easy and catches up with some reading.

MONKEE MAGIC

In America, one of the strangest pop music combinations hit the road when teen heroes the Monkees booked the Jimi Hendrix Experience as their support act. Monkee Micky Dolenz had seen Hendrix's group perform and persuaded his bandmates to book the British trio for their tour, which kicked off in Jacksonville, Florida, on July 8.

When the Monkees' young fans – and their parents – complained about Hendrix's wild onstage antics, Peter Tork observed, "There's poor Jimi and the kids go, 'We want the Monkees!' It didn't cross anybody's mind that it wasn't gonna fly." By the time the tour reached Forest Hills Stadium in New York, on Sunday, July 16, Hendrix had had enough of being screamed at by irate Monkees fans. "The yelling got so bad that he walked off stage," recalls Mike Nesmith. "He was in the middle of a number, threw his guitar down, flipped everyone the bird, and said, 'Fuck you!' and walked off. I turned to Micky and said, 'Good for him.'"

Later, Hendrix told the music press, "We decided it was just the wrong audience. I think they're replacing me with Mickey Mouse." In an effort to get some mileage out of the situation – and convince people that Hendrix had not been sacked from the tour – manager Chas Chandler devised a story that the right-wing Daughters of the American Rvolution had campaigned to ban Hendrix because his act was 'obscene'. Despite the fact that nobody in that organization had ever seen Hendrix or complained, the story made the newspapers. Chandler waited for a reaction: "We expected to get sued by the Daughters of the American Revolution. But we never were."

AUGUST

Offering solidarity with the briefly imprisoned Rolling Stones, Mick Jagger and Keith Richards, the Who issued versions of 'The Last Time' and 'Under My Thumb'. The writing on the record read, "The Who, in support of Mick and Keith", and royalties from sales went to aid the Stones' legal costs. The songs were recorded in June, when the pair were in prison, and the Who told the world that they would carry on recording songs by Jagger and Richards "for as long as they are in jail, in order to keep their work before the public".

Released from prison and back in the studio the Rolling Stones released 'We Love You', which, according to *NME*'s August 12 issue, was as "simple as 'All You Need Is Love'" but went on to say, "the musical holocaust surrounding it is so cleverly produced you will be able to listen to it again and again and still find new ideas." At the same time, US psychedelic group Moby Grape put out their single 'Omaha' and the same music paper declared, "This is a sensational new San Franciscan group which performs r-and-b, c-and-w, rock 'n' roll and psychedelia – all with equal dexterity."

Newly formed Fleetwood Mac (Mick Fleetwood, Peter Green, Jeremy Spencer and Bob Brunning) made their debut at the Windsor Jazz and Blues Festival during the weekend of August 12 and 13. The next weekend's festival attracted Cream, Jeff Beck, Donovan and the Move. But *NME*'s reporter was more interested in the fans than the music. "Out in the grounds beyond the stage, the hippies reeled around and smiled and showed off their coloured robes. Windsor was a nice try but not an answer to Monterey."

Pink Floyd's debut album, *The Piper at the Gates of Dawn*, which featured a kaleidoscopic cover shot of the group by photographer Vic Singh, was seen by some to represent an LSD trip. Photographer Gered Mankowitz takes the view that the image was chosen, "because they didn't have a lot of good band photographs and they had used what they had to create that multi-imaging effect".

While the album shot to No.6 in the UK chart, the band did not impress an *NME* reader named G. Rollason, from Coventry. "Having seen Pink Floyd I am bewildered. Can someone please explain what this psychedelic crap is all about?" They were not received any better in America, where they were signed to EMI's sister company, Capitol Records. "Floyd were not welcomed with any great enthusiasm and were put out on Tower, which was a sort of their secondary label," says Dan Davis. "They were a progressive or underground act – one of the very few at Capitol back then – and the A&R people never really understood the new music that was arriving in the mid-sixties."

America was still rife with anti-Vietnam-war protests. Folk singer Joan Baez suffered at the hands of the Daughters of the American Revolution when they objected to her anti-war stance. The organization had Baez banned from performing in the Constitution Hall in

Opposite above: The bodies of 39-year-old playwright Joe Orton and his killer Keith Halliwell – who committed suicide – were discovered at Orton's Islington home on August 9, 1967.

Opposite below: Pink Floyd's first album cover – a trip or a trick?

Overleaf: Paul McCartney (left) and Rolling Stone Mick Jagger have a "first class" smoke as they wait for the train to leave London's Euston station on August 25, 1967.

ROCK THE BOAT

Britain's first pirate radio station started broadcasting in March 1964, when *Radio Caroline* was moored off the Essex coast. In the same year, Radio Atlanta and Radio London began. Within three years, there were an estimated 21 pirate radio stations broadcasting from international waters, outside Britain's three-mile limit, to a reported daily audience of more than 10 million people.

At midnight on August 14, the British Labour Government introduced the Marine Offences Act into law, citing that a host of national radio stations throughout Europe had suffered interference from the pirate stations. Pirate radio was dead. Only the original pirate station, Radio Caroline, was allowed to continue, and it announced it would move its offices from London to Amsterdam and Paris.

Now a broadcaster on BBC Essex, Dave Monk was a 16-year-old "pirate" fan in 1967. "I listened to Caroline religiously even after all the other closed down. There was something dashing about the sticking two fingers up at the legislation."

According to Johnnie Walker, who joined Radio Caroline from Radio England in 1966, a daily tender service brought records out to the ship. However, "After August 1967, record companies could have nothing to do with us – any company that did send records to Caroline would have been breaking the law."

Peter Robinson, a journalist and music promoter in Brighton, was a visitor to both Radios Caroline and London as part of his journalism course. "We took a tender from Harwich and I came back looking over my shoulder in case anyone was about to apprehend me. It was very exciting – we saw Dave Cash, Kenny Everett and Tony Blackburn in action."

Another visitor to Radio Caroline was Peter Asher with his singing partner Gordon Waller. Asher recalls waiting on a beach in Essex to be collected. "A boat would be there and they would zip you out to the ship and we spent the day there doing interviews. It was very exciting because you felt you were evading the security forces – and it sounded a lot better than Radio Luxembourg."

Johnnie Walker remembers that Peter and Gordon were probably one of the few acts that made the trip out to the ship. "Not that many artists came out as it involved a train from London, a taxi to Harwich or Folkestone and then the tender out to Caroline, which took about 90 minutes each way and left most people feeling sick."

However, this all came to an end with the passing of the new law. The *Sun* newspaper wrote an orbituary. "Exit the pirates. They gave a lot of pleasure to their fans and made a lot of money. They had to go because anarchy on radio wavelengths is not tolerable."

In response, the fans made their feelings known. Newspaper reports claimed that 1,000 teenagers, "besieged Liverpool Street station in protest against the closure of the pirate radio stations" and added that "youths and girls ran riot as disc jockeys and staff [from the pirate stations] arrived at the station." It was claimed that crash barriers were pushed over and train windows were smashed. DJ Pete Drummond said, "We hoped there would be a bit of a demonstration ... but this is awful."

Washington, D.C., and Baez suggested that the Daughters had, "a different idea of freedom from what I have, and I think I threaten theirs".

On August 25, the Beatles – with their wives and girlfriends in tow – plus Mick Jagger and Marianne Faithfull, took the train to Bangor, north Wales, to attend a teaching seminar held by the Maharishi Mahesh Yogi. While they were there they received the news that Brian Epstein had been found dead on August 27. Epstein's funeral took place two days later. It was a private family affair, which none of his acts – including the Beatles – attended.

During a visit to London, Frank Zappa spoke out about Britain's response to the American West Coast scene. "From what I can see so far, the people in Britain have no idea what a real San Franciscan love-in is like. There is a popularization of the flower-power movement. I believe in love – not phoney bullshit love."

The end of August brought with it the last episode of the popular American TV series *The Fugitive* after 120 episodes. Starring David Jansen as the falsely convicted murderer Dr. Richard Kimble, the series ran from 1963. The show's finale was watched by more than 78 million viewers.

Left: George Harrison strums a guitar as he strolls his way through the hippie-haven of Haight Ashbury in San Francisco in August 1967, accompanied by the Beatles' press officer Derek Taylor.

Overleaf top left: On his way to Bangor Paul McCartney gets a reassuring hand from a fan at Euston station.

Overleaf below left: Paul McCartney (left) Ringo Starr (centre) and John Lennon listen to the words of the Maharishi Mahesh Yogi during the trip to Bangor.

Overleaf right: Say it with flowers – The Beatles and the Maharishi Mahesh Yogi at the Meditation conference in Bangor.

SEPTEMBER

The people of Sweden woke on September 3 to a new traffic system. The country switched to driving on the right-hand side of the road after more than 50 years of left-side driving. The switch involved reorganizing one-way streets, moving bus stops and changing more than 360,000 road signs.

A day later, September 4, US Marines attacked two provinces in Vietnam in Operation Swift. The four-day battle left 144 US servicemen, and 376 North Vietnamese, dead.

Over in Gibraltar, the nation was voting for its future as it held a referendum on September 10 to decide whether to remain as part of Great Britain. With a 95 per cent turnout, over 99 per cent of the citizens decided to retain British sovereignty, which dated back to 1713.

On September 16, Sir Malcolm Sargent made his final appearance at the Henry Wood Promenade Concerts after serving as conductor at London's Royal Albert Hall since 1947. Sargent, known as "Flash Harry" because of his impeccable appearance, joined his successor, Colin Davis, to wave a final farewell on the famous Last Night of the Proms. He died two weeks later, aged 72.

Jim Morrison and the Doors ran into trouble on September 17 when they appeared on *The Ed Sullivan TV Show* to promote their chart-topping single 'Light My Fire'. Producers wanted Morrison to change the line, "Girl, we couldn't get much higher", and, although the singer agreed, when it came to the broadcast he sang the original line. Like the Stones before them, the Doors were never invited back.

Below: The Beatles model a range of matching cardigans to meet a Japanese visitor to Abbey Road in September 1967.

Right: A windswept John Lennon looks out over the West country while filming *Magical Mystery Tour*.

Melody Maker's 1967 Poll Awards lauded Sgt. Pepper as the Best UK LP, ahead of Jimi Hendrix's Are You Experienced, with Procol Harum's 'A Whiter Shade Of Pale' voted Best UK Single. The Beatles' 'Strawberry Fields Forever' came second. The award for Best International Group went to the Beatles, ahead of the Beach Boys and the Monkees.

On September 20, Britain's newest liner, the QEII, was launched on Clydebank in Scotland by Queen Elizabeth II. The ship weighed 58,000 tons and boasted 1,000 passenger cabins.

At the movies, Arthur Penn's violent film Bonnie and Clyde opened with Warren Beatty and Faye Dunaway in the lead roles. The film's 30s-themed outfits, featuring berets and "gangster" suits, started a fashion trend.

Frank Zappa and his Mothers of Invention took over London's prestigious Royal Albert Hall on September 23 for a concert with the London Symphony Orchestra. The show got mixed reviews from the music press. However, Melody Maker decided it was, "one of the greatest live performances to have shaken this earth on

Opposite: The Magical Mystery Tour started in September 1967 and John Lennon (left) and George Harrison are forced to stand behind Ringo Starr and Paul McCartney as the coach trip gets under way.

Above and **Below:** Faye Dunaway starred in Bonnie and Clyde as the American bank robber and sexy gangster's moll Bonnie Parker.

Left: New on Radio 1, disc jockeys (left to right) Pete Brady, Mike A'Hearn, Dave Cash, Kenny Everett and Duncan Johnson gather round.

Right: George Harrison pictured at EMI's Abbey Road studio as the Beatles set about creating the music for *Magical Mystery Tour*.

Overleft: There's work to be done and John Lennon (left) and Paul McCartney are in the studio to produce the *Magical Mystery Tour* EP.

this side of the Atlantic for a long a time". *NME* disagreed: "An entire concert of biting ridicule, both verbal and musical – however well done – is just a bore."

Following in the footsteps of *Thunderbirds*, Gerry and Sylvia Anderson launched *Captain Scarlet and the Mysterons*, which was first broadcast on September 29. Using marionette puppets, scale-model sets and special effects, the creators filmed the shows in what they called "Supermarionation" and sold them to more than 40 countries.

A month after the legal closure of pirate radio stations, the BBC opened up their new radio format on September 30 with the previous Light Programme splitting to form Radio 1 and Radio 2. Ahead of the launch, the controller at Radio 1, Robin Scott, outlined his plan for the new station to the *Sun* newspaper. "We will present

live warm-hearted swinging programmes. We cannot deny we will use some of the techniques of the commercial stations." Then, in a putdown for any girls who aspired to join the station, he added, "We will include anyone with a regular British accent if he is good at the job."

When it finally started, at 7am on a Saturday morning, Radio 1 featured DJ Tony Blackburn – who played the Move's 'Flowers In The Rain' as the first record. At 10am, Keith Sykes took over, then Emperor Rosko ran through from noon until 2pm, before Chris Denning's one-hour show. Pete Murray followed at 3pm, Pete Brady at 4pm, and *Country Meets Folk* at 5.30pm until *Scene and Heard* – boasting an interview with George Harrison – ran until 7.30pm. That was when Radio 2 took over the airwaves for two and a half hours with Pete Murray and guests Geno Washington, Manfred Mann and live jazz

from Cleo Laine and Acker Bilk.

The reaction to the new station was mixed, with *NME* reporting, "It was like a curate's egg – good in parts. Radio 1 is youthful, fast moving, pop-laden and a complete reversal of Auntie BBC's former image ... a mild success with considerable room for improvement."

For Peter Robinson, now head of Dome Records, Radio 1 was a welcome arrival. "It made a big difference. As much as people mourned the disappearance of the pirate stations, once Radio 1 started they did play music that would not have been on the Light Programme." Author David Roberts was equally impressed: "Radio was an event and the BBC were very clever by saying what was coming and we teenagers looked forward to things. And there were exciting DJs from the pirate ships."

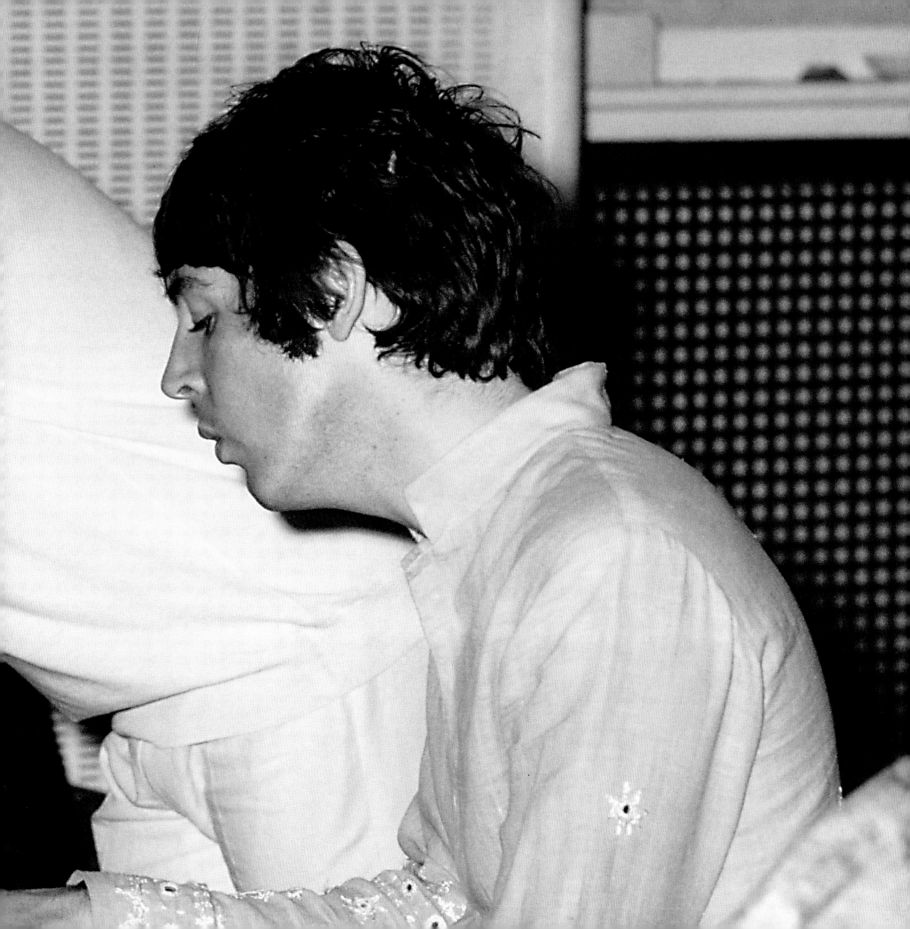

OCTOBER

October 1967 began with the death of folk legend Woody Guthrie. The man who wrote 'This Land Is Your Land' – and inspired Robert Zimmerman to become Bob Dylan – died in New York on October 3, aged 55.

Two months after their final concert at Candlestick Park, San Francisco, the Beatles refused a major offer to go back on stage when on October 7 promoter Sid Bernstein offered them $1 million to play two concerts in one day at Shea Stadium, New York. The band would also receive income from the sale of the shows to television networks.

Tony Bramwell, general manager of the Saville Theatre, holds the view that if the Beatles were to perform live once more it would have been at the theatre once owned by Brian Epstein. "There would have been a chance of them playing the Saville if anyone could have worked out a way of doing it technically, but the sound systemss simply didn't exist back then."

Pink Floyd headlined the Saville Theatre on October 7, with *NME* pointing out that "the beautiful people and the hippies turned up in their shawls, embroidered jackets, Indian head bands and beads", to see the band, who offered "weird lighting, floating patterns and waving silhouettes".

Before the month was out, Pink Floyd were in America to play at San Francisco's Winterland ballroom, where they were billed as "The Light Kings of England", but, according to band member Nick Mason, things did not go well: "Jet-lagged on arrival, we were swept into a chaotic series of dates, under-financed, under-equipped and overwhelmed," and the tour was eventually cancelled when Syd Barrett

refused to lip-synch during an appearance on the *American Bandstand* TV show.

On October 9, Marxist revolutionary Ernesto "Che" Guevara was shot and killed in Bolivia as he tried to rally support to overthrow President Barrientos. The man born Ernesto Guevara, in Argentina, was 39 years old when he died and his remains lay undiscovered in Bolivia for 30 years before being retrieved and taken to Cuba for burial.

The following day, the Move were in the High Court in London, where they apologized to Prime Minister Harold Wilson for using a postcard depicting a nude caricature of Wilson lying in bed to promote their single 'Flowers In the Rain'. Wilson sued the band for libel and they were forced to hand over all royalties from the sales of the song (estimated to be around £10,000) to the Spastics Society and Stoke Mandeville Hospital.

October 12 saw the publication of a provocative new book. *The Naked Ape* by zoologist Dr Desmond Morris looked at humans as a species compared to other animals. It was translated into 23 languages but it was not without controversy as a New York District

Right: George Harrison (left) and John Lennon (right) pose with David Frost before their appearance on his TV show in October 1967.

Opposite: The face of Argentinian revolutionary Che Guevara, who was killed in Bolivia, went on to adorn students' walls all around the globe.

banned it from school libraries.

On October 17, as the Beatles attended a memorial service for Brian Epstein at the New London Synagogue, a controversial new musical opened off Broadway in New York's Anspacher Theater. *Hair*, dubbed the first rock musical, included nudity and swearing and featured a racially integrated cast. For Paul Gambaccini, the show was "one of the transformative musicals of my lifetime" and Tim Rice agrees: "The idea of a rock musical was very exciting and when we did *Jesus Christ Superstar* we were definitely influenced by *Hair*."

All four Beatles were together again on October 18, when, with wives and girlfriends on their arms, they attended the premiere of the film *How I Won the War*, starring John Lennon as Musketeer Gripweed alongside popular singer and actor Michael Crawford.

In the same week, the controversial film *To Sir With Love* opened in London. Focusing

Right: *Hair* brought the concept of the rock musical to life in a New York theatre.

Above: Paul McCartney (left) and George Harrison (right) with girlfriends, make their way to the premiere of *How I Won The War*.

on social and racial issues in an east London school, the movie starred Sidney Poitier, Judy Geeson and Lulu, whose version of the theme song became a million-selling US No.1.

Britain was also busy introducing new laws this month with the Abortion Bill being passed by Parliament and two new motoring laws being introduced as part of British Road Safety Act. The Abortion Bill allowed operations to be carried out legally by licensed practitioners and for free on the National Health Service. At the same time, all new cars in Britain had to be fitted with seat belts – although the law did not require drivers to use them. The breathalyser was introduced to reduce drinking and driving. Dave Monk's

OCTOBER NUMBER ONES

SINGLES

'The Last Waltz'
– Engelbert Humperdinck (UK)

'Massachusetts'
– the Bee Gees (UK)

'The Letter'
– the Box Tops (US)

'To Sir With Love'
– Lulu (US)

ALBUMS

Sgt. Pepper's Lonely Hearts Club Band – the Beatles

Sgt. Pepper's Lonely Hearts Club Band – the Beatles (US)

Ode To Billie Joe
– Bobbie Gentry (US)

Diana Ross and The Supremes: Greatest Hits – Diana Ross and the Supremes (US)

Below: Paul McCartney on his way into the New London Synagogue for the memorial service for Brian Epstein.

Right: Tens of thousands of demonstrators assembled at the Lincoln Memorial in Washington, D.C. to voice their protests against the war in Vietnam.

parents ran a pub and he recalls them worrying about the impact the new law might have on business. "But it made no difference at all. People still came in and got smashed and drove home – sometimes with a local police escort. Nobody took it seriously to start with."

Welsh singing sensation Tom Jones became a millionaire when he signed up for 13 weeks' work singing for his supper at the Flamingo Casino, Las Vegas. It was the highest fee ever paid to a British singer in America.

On October 21, more anti-Vietnam war protesters turned out in force, following the arrest of America's first lady of folk, Joan Baez – plus 123 other protesters – at an anti-draft demonstration at an Armed Forces centre in California. Over 100,000 people joined the "March on the Pentagon to Confront War Makers" rally at the Lincoln Memorial in Washington, D.C. Novelist and journalist Norman Mailer was among those arrested when they marched on the Pentagon building.

On October 22, the Who topped the bill at the Saville Theatre in what Record Mirror described as "an ear-splitting, mind-blowing, supersonic-sounding sensation". According to general manager Tony Bramwell, the bands didn't get paid a lot for their efforts. "All the bands we booked – Floyd, Hendrix, Cream, Traffic – were in England and cheap. Hendrix we paid £75. Cream and the Who we paid around £50. They all loved playing there as it was the only venue that was a real theatre."

" LSD enables you to see a lot of possibilities that you may not have noticed before. But it isn't the answer. "

GEORGE HARRISON

NOVEMBER

On November 7, Carl B. Stokes was voted into power in Cleveland, Ohio – the country's first African-American mayor of a major US city. On the same day, President Lyndon B. Johnson signed the Public Broadcasting Act and created the Corporation for Public Broadcasting, which was charged with making non-commercial, high-quality radio and television accessible throughout the US.

Meanwhile, in the Soviet Union, the nation was celebrating the 50th anniversary of the great October Socialist Revolution of 1917, an event that ended the rule of the Romanov dynasty and saw Vladimir Lenin lead a workers' revolution and seize power.

On October 9, the first edition of *Rolling Stone* magazine was published in America. The brainchild of University of California drop-out Jann Wenner, the first issue featured a cover photograph of John Lennon, taken during the shooting of the film *How I Won The War*. The magazine's title was inspired by a Muddy Waters song and the first edition came with a freebie roach clip.

ROLLING STONE

MFP

NOVEMBER 9, 1967
VOL. I, NO. 1

OUR PRICE: TWENTY-FIVE CENTS

IN THIS ISSUE:

DONOVAN: An incredible Rolling Stone Interview with this manchild of magic .... Page 14

GRATEFUL DEAD: A photographic look at a rock and roll group after a dope bust .... Page 8

BYRD IS FLIPPED: Jim McGuinn kicks out David Crosby .... Page 4

RALPH GLEASON: The color bar on American television ..... Page 11

Recognize Private Gripeweed? He's actually John Lennon in Richard Lester's new film, How I Won the War. An illustrated special preview of the movie begins on page 16.

Tom Rounds Quits KFRC

Tom Rounds, KFRC Program Director, has resigned. No immediate date has been set for his departure from the station. Rounds quit to assume the direction of Charlatan Productions, an L.A. based film company experimenting in the contemporary pop film.

Rounds spent seven years as Program Director of KPOI in Hawaii before coming to San Francisco in 1966. He successfully effected the tight format which made KFRC the number one station in San Francisco.

Les Turpin, former program director of KGB in San Diego will replace Tom Rounds at KFRC. Turpin has spent the last year as a consultant in the Drake-Chenault programming service.

The new appointment could mean a tightening up of programming policies. Rounds liberalization of KFRC's play-list may well become more restricted.

THE HIGH COST OF MUSIC AND LOVE: WHERE'S THE MONEY FROM MONTEREY?

BY MICHAEL LYDON

A weekend of "music, love, and flowers" can be done for a song (plus cost) or can be done at a cost (plus songs). The Monterey International Pop Festival, a non-profit, charity event, was, despite its own protestations, of the second sort: a damn extravagant three days.

The Festival's net profit at the end of August, the last date of accounting, was $211,451. The costs of the weekend were $290,233. Had it not been for the profit from the sale of television rights to ABC-TV of $288,843, the whole operation would have ended up a neat $77,392 in the red.

The Festival planned to have all the artists, while in Monterey, submit ideas for use of the proceeds.

In the confusion the plan miscarried and the decision on where the profits should go has still not been finally made.

So far only $50,000 has definitely been been allocated to anyone: to a unit of the New York City Youth Board which will set up classes for many ghetto children to learn music on guitars donated by Fender. Paul Simon, a Festival governor, will personally over see the program.

Plans to give more money to the Negro College Fund for college scholarships is now being discussed; another idea is a sum between ten and twenty thousand for the Monterey Symphony.

However worthy these plans, they are considerably less daring and innovative than the projects mentioned in the spring: the Diggers, pop conferences, and any project which would "tend to further national interest in and knowledge and enjoyment of popular music." The present plans suggest that the Board of Governors, unable or unwilling to make their grandiose schemes reality, fell back on traditional charity.

The Board of Governors did decide that the money would be given out in a small number of large sums. This has meant, for instance, that the John Edwards Memorial Foundation, a folk music archive at the University of California at Los Angeles, had its small request overlooked.

In ironic fact, what happened at the Festival and its financial affairs looks in many ways like the traditional Charity Ball in hippie drag.

The overhead was high and the net was low. "For every dollar spent, there was a reason," says Derek Taylor, the Festival's PR man and one of its original officers.

Yet many of the Festival's expenses, however reasonable to Taylor, seem out of keeping with its announced spirit. The Festival management, with amateurish good will, lavished generosity on their friends.

● Producer Lou Adler was able to find a spot in the show for his own property, Johnny Rivers; Paul Simon for his friend, English folk singer Beverly; John Phillips for the Group Without A Name and Scott MacKenzie. None of them had the musical

Airplane high, but no new LP release

Jefferson Airplane has been taking more than a month to record their new album for RCA Victor. In a recording period of five weeks only five sides have been completed. No definite release date has been set.

Their usual recording schedule in Los Angeles begins at 11:00 p.m. in the evening and extends through six or seven in the morning. When they're not in the studios, they stay at a fabulous pink mansion which rents for $5,000 a month. The Beatles stayed at the house on their last American tour.

The house has two swimming pools and a variety of recreational facilities. It's a small small little paradise in the hills above Hollywood. Maybe suntans and guitars don't make it together.

status for an international pop music festival.

It is ironic that the Rivers and the rest appeared "free," but the money it cost the Festival to get them to Monterey and back, feed them, put them up (Beverly

—Continued on Page 7

Opposite left: A week after being elected, Carl B. Stokes is sworn in as Mayor of Cleveland.

Opposite right: The first issue of *Rolling Stone* magazine featured John Lennon on the cover.

Right: The wreckage of Otis Redding's plane is recovered from Lake Monona in Wisconsin, December 1967.

The magazine's arrival, together with other new artistic events, made an impact, according to Dan Davis, a youthful Capitol Records employee at the time. "The opening of *Hair* and the start of *Rolling Stone* magazine truly legitimized rock in the minds of many of my elders at Capitol."

On November 10, the second album from British supergroup Cream, *Disraeli Gears*, a top five hit in both the US and the UK, was released and was declared by *Melody Maker* as, "a propelling package of incredible superpower", which featured " hypnotic musical journeys".

On November 17, the same day Paris hosted a two-day "Love-In" at the Palais de Sport – featuring Soft Machine and Dandelion's Chariot – US President Johnson gave the people of America an update on the war in Vietnam. He announced: "We are inflicting greater losses than we are taking … we are making progress."

On the same day, the Beatles changed the name of their business to Apple Music Limited. A day later, British Prime Minister Harold Wilson devalued the pound by lowering the dollar exchange rate from $2.80 to $2.40. He told the nation that it was the only way to tackle Britain's economic problems and added that the "pound in your pocket" would not be affected.

NOVEMBER NUMBER ONES

SINGLES (UK)

'Massachusetts' – the Bee Gees (UK)

'Baby Now That I've Found You'
– the Foundations (UK)

'Let the Heartaches Begin'
– Long John Baldry (UK)

'To Sir With Love' – Lulu (US)

'Incense and Peppermint'
– Strawberry Alarm Clock (US)

ALBUMS

Sgt. Pepper's Lonely Hearts Club Band
– the Beatles (UK)

The Sound of Music (UK)

Diana Ross and the Supremes: Greatest Hits – Diana Ross and the Supremes (US)

'HELLO GOODBYE'

The Beatles' third single in 1967 was released on November 24 and by Christmas it had topped the charts in both the UK and the US. 'Hello Goodbye', which started out with the working title 'Hello Hello', was recorded on October 2, when 15 takes were captured at Abbey Road Studios, and was finished after three more sessions during the same month.

The Beatles started work on the song chosen as the B-side – Lennon's 'I Am The Walrus' – in early September, a little over a week after Brian Epstein's death. Seventeen takes were completed in two days. The song was finished on September 29. George Martin described the recording of 'I Am The Walrus' as "Organized chaos ... I'm proud of that".

Reviewing the Beatles' fourth UK Christmas No.1 (they had topped the charts at Yuletide every year since 1963, except 1966, when there wasn't a Beatles single) *Melody Maker* concluded, "It's gentle Beatles this time with their new Christmas number one, keeping the realms of pop within boundaries of insanity, being as witty and as subtle as ever." However, not all was well with the record as the BBC banned 'I Am The Walrus' because of the line about the girl who let her "knickers down". Lennon responded: "We chose the word 'knickers' because it is a lovely expressive word. It rolls off the tongue."

There were further concerns, however, when the promotional film for 'Hello Goodbye', which featured the Beatles in their *Sgt. Pepper* outfits, on stage at the Saville Theatre "performing" the song, was banned by the Musicians' Union. As the viola players who were on the record were not in the film, and it was obvious the Beatles were miming, the video contravened the Union's ban on miming. The promo was not allowed to be shown on televisions in the UK.

On November 28, the Beatles assembled at Abbey Road Studios to make their fifth fan club record. It would be their last. Alongside messages and jokes, the disc included the title track, 'Christmas Time (Is Here Again)', which was written by all four Beatles. A rarity.

" THE FOUR OF US HAVE GOT ALMOST ANYTHING MONEY CAN BUY. BUT THE THINGS YOU BUY MEAN NOTHING AFTER A TIME. "

RINGO STARR

DECEMBER

The Monkees continued their domination of the American charts when the album *Pisces, Aquarius, Capricorn, and Jones Ltd,* reached No.1 on December 2. The album followed the chart-topping success of *The Monkees, More of the Monkees* and *Headquarters.* On the same day, the single 'Daydream Believer' also topped the US chart, where it stayed until the New Year.

On December 4, in South Africa, surgeon Dr Christian Barnard performed the world's first heart transplant in Cape Town. Barnard removed the heart from Denise Darvall, a young woman killed in an accident, and transplanted it into shopkeeper Louis Washkansky in a revolutionary operation. Washkansky lived for a further 18 days after the pioneering surgery. Jann Haworth's memory of the operation is of "watching news about the impossible – the world waited for him to live ... watched and listened to a life as never before".

Having launched their new company, the Beatles opened their Apple Boutique in London's Baker Street on December 7. An Anglo-Dutch design team known as the Fool received £100,000 from the Beatles to create and stock the shop. It lasted until July 1968, when staff were told to give everything away to customers. Lennon later commented on the whole ordeal: "It ended up with Apple and all this junk and the Fool and all those stupid clothes and all that."

The Beatles' main rivals in the world of rock, the Rolling Stones, surprised everybody by releasing a second album in 1967. *Their Satanic Majesties Request* was released on December 8. *NME* described it as "the trip to infinity – the journey to the dark spaces between the stars and beyond".

Described by Keith Richards as "a bit of flim-flam", *Their Satanic Majesties Request* did herald a new style of album sleeve – a 3D design. Michael Cooper, the man who photographed the *Sgt. pepper* sleeve, was responsible. Gered Mankowitz had been the main photographer for

the Stones, but, as the band were splitting from manager Andrew Loog Oldham, Mankowitz sensed that a change was in the air. "I knew that I was being replaced and that Michael Cooper was taking my position. I didn't find him friendly or particularly nice, but the Stones, in particular Mick and Keith, were becoming very cliquey. It was all revolving around drugs and Cooper and Robert Fraser and those people."

However, when Mankowitz saw what Cooper had produced for the latest Stones album, he was impressed. "When I saw *Satanic* I was in awe of the three-dimensional lenticular cover, which I thought was fabulous. But I was also pissed off because I had discovered lenticular postcards in New York in 1965 and bought one and showed it to the Stones."

A week after the album's release, Brian Jones had his nine-month prison sentence from October for drug possession quashed. It was replaced with a £100 fine and three years' probation after psychiatrists warned that he had suicidal tendencies.

On December 10, American soul singer Otis Redding was killed when his plane crashed into

Above: The Stones' innovative cover for *Their Satanic Majesties Request,* created by the man who photographed *Sgt. Pepper.*

Opposite: The end of 1967 and Ringo Starr is looking ahead to a career in the movies and acting with the likes of Marlon Brando and Richard Burton.

DECEMBER NUMBER ONES

SINGLES

'Hello Goodbye' - the Beatles (UK)
'Daydream Believer' - the Monkees (US)
'Hello Goodbye' - the Beatles (US)

ALBUMS

The Sound of Music (UK)
Sgt. Pepper's Lonely Hearts Club Band
- the Beatles (UK)
Pisces, Aquarius, Capricorn & Jones Ltd
- the Monkees (US)

MAGICAL MYSTERY TOUR

Even for the Beatles, the idea of producing a bunch of new songs and segueing them into a film was ambitious. *Magical Mystery Tour* was, according to Tony Bramwell, McCartney's idea. "Paul went to Vegas and on the way home somewhere in mid-air, his active mind dreamed up another wildly innovative concept: a magical mystery tour."

"I'm not sure whose idea *Magical Mystery Tour* was," McCartney admitted. "It could have been mine but I'm not sure I want to take the blame for it." Ringo Starr is adamant. "*Magical Mystery Tour* was Paul's idea. Paul had a piece of paper – just a blank piece of white paper with a circle on it. The plan was: 'We start here – and we've got to do something here'. We filled it in as we went along."

Lennon summed up the idea as being about "a bunch of common people on a coach tour around everywhere, really, and things happen to them".

On September 5, 1967, four days after the death of manager Epstein, all four Beatles united at McCartney's house to discuss their future plans. Between them they decided to forge ahead with the Magical Mystery Tour idea.

Within two weeks, the Beatles were back at Abbey Road Studios to begin working on the title track, which was finished in early May. The rest of the album's tracks were not started until August 22, when the group returned to the *Magical Mystery Tour* project, recording 'Your Mother Should Know' in Chappell Studios. Work on 'I Am the Walrus', 'The Fool On The Hill', 'Blue Jay Way' and 'Flying' continued up until early September, when film-making took over.

Setting off on September 11, the psychedelic coach hired for the *Magical Mystery Tour* collected McCartney from near Baker Street station, before picking up his bandmates in Virginia Water and Surrey and then travelling onwards to Teignmouth, Devon. Over the next four days, the Beatles, with assorted guests, friends and performers, including Ivor Cutler, Nat Jackley, Jessie Robbins and George Claydon, travelled through Devon and Cornwall, filming as they went.

After a day at Abbey Road recording 'Your Mother Should Know', the Beatles were back filming on September 18 and this time it was at Paul Raymond's Revue Bar in Soho, with the Bonzo Dog Doo-Dah Band and stripper Jane Carson for company. For the following six days the Beatles moved to RAF West Malling in Maidstone, Kent, to film "interior" sequences, including the grand-finale scene featuring members of the Peggy Spencer Formation Dancing Team and two dozen Women's Royal Air Force cadets.

With the filming all but complete, the Beatles returned to Abbey Road and from September through to November they completed the six tracks that would appear on the *Magical Mystery Tour* double-EP package, which cost 19s. 6d and came complete with a 28-page colour booklet. George Martin admitted, "*Magical Mystery Tour* was terribly organized. It's amazing anything ever came out of it. They were in their random period. It was chaotic."

Magical Mystery Tour was issued in the UK on December 8. The US market was not accustomed to EPs, so Capitol Records added 'Hello Goodbye', 'Strawberry Fields Forever', 'Penny Lane', 'Baby You're A Rich Man' and 'All You Need Is Love' to the other six tracks. It went to No.1 and sold more than three million copies.

As the double EP climbed the UK singles chart – it peaked at No.2 – the critics were united in favour of the latest Beatles offering. *Melody Maker*'s Bob Dawbarn declared that they were "six tracks which no other pop group in the world could begin to approach for originality combined with the popular touch", while *NME*'s Nick Logan suggested: "The Beatles are at it again, stretching pop music to its limits on beautiful sound canvases ... a magical mystery tour of sounds fantastic, sounds unbelievable. This is *Sgt. Pepper* and beyond, heading for marvellous places."

On December 21, four days before *Magical Mystery Tour* was set to be broadcast on the BBC, the Beatles held a fancy-dress party for the cast and crew of the film. Lennon went dressed as a Teddy boy and McCartney and his girlfriend Jane Asher arrived as a pearly king and queen.

After six weeks of editing, *Magical Mystery Tour* was ready to air. It was finally broadcast on BBC TV at 8.35pm on December 26. The 55-minute Technicolor film – which was aired on TV in black and white – attracted an estimated viewing audience of 13 million. The critics were not amused. The *Daily Express* claimed they "had never seen such blatant rubbish", while James Green at the *London Evening News* remarked, "I watched it. There was precious little magic and the only mystery was how the BBC came to buy it."

The music press was kinder. *NME* commented, "the film is never dull". *Melody Maker* suggested the show "was not so much a flop as a mass audience flop, even though it might have been a Beatles triumph. You can't take Joe Public and pitch him into the deep-end of the Beatles' world."

During the year, the Beatles had set new standards in recording and survived the advance of the "prog" movement from America as well as the arrival of a new teenage phenomenon. 1967 came to a conclusion just as previous years had: the Beatles were once again at the top of the singles charts in the UK and the US and back at No.1 on the British album chart – where they belonged.

Previous page: Behind the scaffolding, work goes on to finish the Beatles' Apple boutique which stood at the junction of Baker Street and Paddington Street in London.

Left: Anglo-French aviation project Concorde 001 being prepared for public view in a hangar in Toulouse in France.

Above: South African surgeon Professor Christian Barnard was the pioneer of heart transplant surgery.

Right: Anne Bancroft and Dustin Hoffman in a scene from the 1967 Oscar-winning film *The Graduate.*

Overleaf, left: Welsh artist Jonathan Hague (right) at his December 1967 exhibition at the Royal Institute Gallery in London with his sponsor John Lennon – and a *Sgt. Pepper* painting from the show.

Overleaf, left, above: The Beatles look on appreciatively as topless dancer Jane Carson performs in Raymond's Revue Bar for a scene from *Magical Mystery Tour.*

Overleaf, left, below: When it came to parking in London Paul McCartney opted for a mini rather than a limo.

Lake Monoma, Wisconsin. Four members of his backing band, the Bar Keys, also died. Three days earlier, the 27-year-old had started work on the song '(Sittin' On) The Dock Of The Bay' and after his death the track was finished by his Stax Studio team. It was released in March 1968 and became Redding's only US No.1 hit.

Six months after a law forbidding interracial marriage in 17 of America's states was finally lifted, *Guess Who's Coming to Dinner* – a film that focused on the engagement of a black man to a white woman – was released. Starring Spencer Tracy, Katherine Hepburn and Sidney Poitier, the film was nominated for eight Academy Awards, winning two – Hepburn for Best Actress and for Best Screenplay.

The 1967 Academy Award for Best Director was won by Mike Nicols for his film *The Graduate*, which opened on December 21. Starring Dustin Hoffman, Anne Bancroft and Katherine Ross, the film's famous soundtrack was written by Paul Simon and Art Garfunkel.

In late 1967, a brand-new plane was rolled out for the first time in Toulouse, France, and British minister Tony Benn announced to the world that the supersonic jet would be called Concorde, despite a number of UK politicians wanting it to be named Concord – a word meaning, ironically, an agreement between peoples.

On December 27, the BBC decided to cancel *Juke Box Jury*, one of British television's longest-running pop music shows. It came to an end after nine years and 1,432 airings. The show began in 1959 and at its peak drew audiences of over 12 million, although, when the Beatles appeared in 1963, the viewing figures spiked to 23 million. The final show was hosted by David Jacobs and featured Pete Murray, Lulu, comedian Eric Sykes and *Magpie* presenter Susan Stranks.

1968

THE YEAR AFTER

As far as popular music was concerned, 1968 arrived with John, Paul, George and Ringo wandering ... but far from lost. There were a host of exciting new avenues for them to explore. The Mop Tops had grown up and were now very much in charge of their own destiny.

The Beatles' involvement in 1968's British No.1 hit singles ran from March to November as 'Lady Madonna' was followed to the top spot in September by 'Hey Jude'. In August, the group had launched Apple Records, as part of the renamed Apple Corps Ltd, and among the first releases were Mary Hopkin's 'Those Were The Days', produced by McCartney, who signed the Welsh singer after her appearance on a TV talent show. Hopkin's debut single eventually replaced 'Hey Jude' in the top spot, before Joe Cocker took over in October with his version of the Beatles' song 'With a Little Help From My Friends'. Finally, McCartney's brother Mike McGear, and his group the Scaffold, reached number one in November with 'Lily The Pink'.

In the midst of this all this Beatles-related activity Cliff Richard returned to No.1 for the first time in three years with 'Congratulations', which was also runner-up in the Eurovision Song Contest. Never to be outdone, the Rolling Stones emerged victorious with their seventh No.1 single – 'Jumpin' Jack Flash'.

Simon and Garfunkel racked up two No.1 albums with *The Graduate* soundtrack and

Bookends, while the flag for the psychedelic/progressive movement was kept at full mast thanks to the No.1 albums from Cream (*Wheels on Fire*), the Doors (*Waiting for the Sun*), the Rascals (*Time Peace*), Big Brother & The Holding Company (*Cheap Thrills*) and Jimi Hendrix (*Electric Ladyland*).

On the US singles chart, only one British act hit number one in 1968 – the Beatles with 'Hey Jude' – while the likes of Herb Alpert ('This Guy's In Love With You'), Hugh Masekela ('Grazing In The Grass') and Jeannie C. Riley ('Harper Valley P.T.A.') shared the crown with Motown act the Supremes ('Love Child') and Marvin Gaye ('I

Heard It Through The Grapevine'), plus Otis Redding's posthumous hit '(Sittin' On) The Dock Of The Bay'.

In the "real world", 1968 began with Alexander Dubček, under the banner of the "Prague Spring", becoming leader of Czechoslovakia. His ambition was to liberalize the country's communist government but, in August, 250,000 Warsaw Pact troops from the Soviet Union, Bulgaria, Hungary and Poland marched in to restore the country to communist rule.

On January 8, Britain's Prime Minister Harold Wilson gave his support to the "I'm Backing Britain" campaign, which was aimed at people working for an extra 30 minutes a day for no extra pay.

February began with the birth of Lisa Marie Presley, the daughter of Elvis and Priscilla, in Memphis and the month ended with the death of singer Frankie Lymon from a heroin overdose.

March saw a mass anti-Vietnam war protest with around 8,000 people gathering in London's Grosvenor Square and ended with Lyndon B. Johnson announcing that he would not stand for re-election as US President. In the same month, Russian cosmonaut Yuri Gargarin – the first man in space in 1961 – was killed in an air crash.

Two major new movies – *2001: A Space Odyssey* and *Planet of the Apes* – opened to great acclaim in April just as Britain saw its first decimal coins as new 5p and 10p pieces were introduced to replace the shilling and florin.

This month saw the world mourn American civil rights activist Martin Luther King, who was shot dead in Memphis on April 4. American Presidential candidate Robert F. Kennedy was shot at the Ambassador Hotel in Los Angeles on June 5; he died the following day.

August 11 was the day when Britain's last steam passenger train service ran, while, towards the end of the month, Boeing rolled out their new 747 aeroplane, which ushered in an age of reliable, safe, economical

Opposite: Welsh singer Mary Hopkin was spotted by Paul McCartney on a TV talent show.

Above: Still at the top of the charts but Paul McCartney (left) and John Lennon contemplate what the future might hold for the Beatles.

international travel.

During the Olympic Games, held in Mexico City from October 12 to 27, US athletes Tommie Smith and John Carlos raised black-power salutes on the medal podium after winning gold and bronze in the men's 200 metres. Both were expelled from the Games.

On November 5, Republican Richard Nixon defeated Hubert Humphrey to become President of the USA and, a week later, America's Ivy League Yale University announced that it would accept female students.

As 1968 came to an close, America's *Apollo 8* astronauts, Frank Borman, Jim Lovell and Williams Anders flew around the moon. On December 24, they became the first humans to see the "dark side of the moon" – five years before Pink Floyd released their multimillion-selling album.

In Britain, 1968 ended – as had 1963, 1964, 1965 and 1967 – with the Beatles on top of the charts with a new album. This time it was *The Beatles* (known as the *White Album*), while in America the group held the No.1 spot at both the beginning (*Magical Mystery Tour*) and end (*White Album*) of the year.

Left: December 1968 and *Apollo 8* sets off on its Christmas-time manned-mission to circle the moon.

Opposite top left: American athletes Tommie Smith (centre) and John Carlos (right) give their Black Power salutes at the 1968 Olympic Games.

Opposite top right: A jubilant Richard M. Nixon is about to become the 37th President of America.

Opposite right: The world caught sight of the first Boeing 747 when the so-called Jumbo Jet was presented to the press and potential customers at the company's plant in Washington state.

INDEX

BIBLIOGRAPHY

Tony Barrow, *John, Paul, George Ringo & Me* (André Deutsch, 2006)

The Beatles, *The Beatles Anthology* (Cassell & Co, 2000)

Tony Bramwell with Rosemary Kingsland, *Magical Mystery Tours: My Life With the Beatles* (Robson Books, 2005)

Eric Clapton, *Eric Clapton: The Autobiography* (Century, 2007)

Ray Coleman, *Brian Epstein: The Man Who Made the Beatles* (Viking, 1989)

Ray Coleman, *Lennon* (Pan Books, 1995)

Ray Coleman, *McCartney Yesterday & Today* (Boxtree, 1995)

Geoff Emerick, *Here, There & Everywhere: My Life Recording the Beatles* (Gotham Books, 2006)

Bob Harris, *Still Whispering After All These Years: My Autobiography* (Michael O'Mara Books, 2001)

Bill Harry, *The Beatles Encyclopedia* (Virgin Books, 2000)

Billy Idol, *Dancing with Myself* (Simon & Schuster, 2015)

Mick Jagger, Keith Richards, Charlie Watts, Ronnie Wood, *According to the Rolling Stones* (Weidenfeld & Nicolson, 2003)

Shawn Levy, *Ready Steady Go!* (Fourth Estate, 2002)

Mark Lewisohn, *The Complete Beatles Recording Sessions* (Hamlyn, 1988)

Greil Marcus, The History of Rock 'N' Roll in Ten Songs (Yale University Press, 2014)

Nick Mason, *Inside Out: A Personal History of Pink Floyd* (Weidenfeld & Nicolson, 2004)

Barry Miles, *The Beatles Diary* (Omnibus Press, 1998)

Graham Nash, *Wild Tales* (Penguin, 2014)

Keith Richards, *Life* (Weidenfeld & Nicolson, 2011)

Johnny Rogan, *Ray Davies: A Complicated Life* (Vintage, 2015)

Brian Southall, *Abbey Road: The Story of the World's Most Famous Recording Studio* (Patrick Stephens, 1982)

Brian Southall, *Jimi Hendrix: Made in England* (Clarksdale, 2012)

Rod Stewart, *Rod: The Autobiography* (Arrow Books, 2013)

Pete Townshend, *Who I Am* (HarperCollins, 2012)

Steve Turner, *A Hard Day's Write* (Carlton, 2005)

John & Gary Walker, *The Walker Brothers: No Regrets* (John Blake, 2005)

ACKNOWLEDGEMENTS

My thanks go to Roland Hall at Carlton Books for his support and ever-helpful suggestions (and short deadlines!)

To all the good people who gave up their time and memories for this book – both are very much appreciated. Thank you.

Also, many thanks to the British Library and its ever-helpful collection of music publications including *Billboard*, *Melody Maker*, *New Musical Express*, which were essential reading.

I am also grateful to these websites: classicbands.com; Relix magazine and Confessions of a Pop addict.

CREDITS

The publishers would like to thank the following sources for their kind permission to reproduce the pictures in this book.

9. Bernie Boston/The Washington Post via Getty Images, 14. David Magnus/REX/Shutterstock, 17. Michael Ochs Archives/Getty Images, 18-19. David Magnus/REX/Shutterstock, 21-22. Mirrorpix, 23. David Redfern/Redferns/Getty Images, 25. Bettmann/Getty Images, 26. Mirrorpix/Kaye, 29. John Williams/BIPs/Getty Images, 30. Mirrorpix, 33. Mirrorpix/Maurice Tibbles, 34. Popperfoto/Getty Images, 36. Mirrorpix (left), 36. CBW/Alamy Stock Photo (right), 37. Ben Martin/The LIFE Images Collection/Getty Images, 38. Tracks Images, 40. Larry Ellis/Express/Getty Images, 41. Mirrorpix, 42. Ilpo Musto/REX/Shutterstock, 43. Michael Ochs Archives/Getty Images (left), 43. Mirrorpix (right), 45. Mal Evans/REX/Shutterstock, 46-47. Tracks Images, 48. David Magnus/REX/Shutterstock, 49. Evening Standard/Getty Images, 50. Clive Limpkin/Daily Express/Getty Images, 51. Chris Walter/Getty Images, 52-53. Larry Ellis/Express/Getty Images, 55. Mirrorpix, 57. CBW/Alamy Stock Photo, 58. Keystone/Getty Images, 59. Heritage Auctions/Bournemouth News/REX/Shutterstock (top), 59. Fred Mott/Evening Standard/Getty Images (bottom), 60. Photograph by Gordon Moore, 61. Shepard Sherbell/Corbis/Corbis via Getty Images, 62-63. © Ted Spiegel/Corbis/Corbis via Getty Images, 65. Mirrorpix, 66. Moore/Express/Getty Images, 67-71. Mirrorpix, 72-73. David Magnus/REX/Shutterstock, 74. Bruce Fleming/Getty Images, 76-77. David Magnus/REX/Shutterstock, 79. Mirrorpix, 81. Christies/PA Archive/PA Images, 83. Laurence Griffiths/Getty Images, 84-85. Photograph by Edgar Zuniga Jr., 86. Ed Kolenovsky AP/Press Association Images, 88. Cummings Archives/Redferns/Getty Images, 89. Mirrorpix/Arthur Sidey, 90. Mirrorpix, 91. Bill Orchard/REX/Shutterstock, 92-93. Koh Hasebe/Shinko Music/Getty Images, 95. Yale Joel/The LIFE Premium Collection/Getty Images, 96. Pictorial Press Ltd/Alamy Stock Photo (top), 96. Yale Joel/The LIFE Premium Collection/Getty Images (centre), 98-99. Elliott Landy/Redferns/Getty Images, 100. Dick Swanson/The LIFE Images Collection/Getty Images, 101. CBW/Alamy Stock Photo, 102. NASA, 103. AP/Press Association Images (top), 103. Mark and Colleen Hayward/Getty Images (bottom), 104. Mirrorpix/NCJ/Topix, 105. Mirrorpix, 107. Avalon/Retna/Photoshot, 108. Paul Sequeira/Getty Images, 108. Blank Archives/Archive Photos/Getty Images (inset), 109. Mick Gold/Redferns/Getty Images, 110. Ed Caraeff/Getty Images, 111. Mirrorpix (top), 111. Private Collection (bottom), 112-114. Mirrorpix, 115. Ian Tyas/Keystone Features/Getty Images, 116. Mirrorpix/George Greenwell, 117. Mirrorpix/Topix, 118-119. Mirrorpix, 120. UPPA/Topfoto.co.uk, 121. Mirrorpix/Doreen Spooner, 122. GAB Archive/Redferns/Getty Images (top left), 122. Mirrorpix/Monte Fresco (top right), 122. Mirrorpix/Russell Cox (bottom), 123. Mirrorpix, 124-125. Marvin Lichtner/The LIFE Images Collection/Getty Images, 126. Mirrorpix, 127. Don Zirkle/AP/Press Association Images, 128-129. Marvin Lichtner/The LIFE Images Collection/Getty Images, 130. Photos 12/Alamy Stock Photo, 131. Bill Zygmant/REX/Shutterstock, 132. Shabtai Tal/GPO via Getty Images, 133. Mirrorpix/Reading Post, 134. Mirrorpix/Sunday People, 136. Ed Kolenovsky/AP/Press Association Images (top), 136. ZUMA Press, Inc./Alamy Stock Photo (bottom left), 136. (bottom right) Mirrorpix/Tom King, 137. Evening Standard/Getty Images, 138-139. David Magnus/REX/Shutterstock, 140. Victor Boyton/AP/Press Association Images, 141. George Stroud/Express/Getty Images, 142. Alain Nogues/Sygma/Sygma via Getty Images, 143. Michael Putland/Getty Images, 144. Mirrorpix, 145. Mirrorpix/Eric Chapman, 146-147. Mark and Colleen Hayward/Redferns/Getty Images, 148. Mirrorpix/Eric Piper (top), 148 Vic Singh Studio/Alamy Stock Photo (bottom), 150-151. Victor Blackman/Express/Getty Images, 152-153. Bettmann/Getty Images, 154. Mirrorpix/Daily Herald (top), 154. (bottom) Mirrorpix/Ann Ward, 155. Mirrorpix, 156. Koh Hasebe/Shinko Music/Getty Images, 157. David Redfern/Redferns/Getty Images, 158. Cummings Archives/Redferns/Getty Images, 159. Warner Bros/Seven Arts/Tatira-Hiller Productions/REX/Shutterstock, 160. Mirrorpix/Daily Herald, 161. Koh Hasebe/Shinko Music/Getty Images, 162-163. Koh Hasebe/Shinko Music/Getty Images, 164. Avalon/Starstock/Photoshot,165. Joseph Scherschel/The LIFE Picture Collection/Getty Images, 166. Ralph Morse/The LIFE Picture Collection/Getty Images, 166. Blank Archives/Getty Images (inset), 167-168. Mirrorpix, 169. Rolls Press/Popperfoto/Getty Images, 171-172 (left) AP/Press Association Images, 172. Granger Historical Picture Archive/Alamy Stock Photo (right), 173. Bettmann/Getty Images, 175. Mirrorpix/Eddie Waters (top), 175. Mark and Colleen Hayward/Getty Images (bottom), 176. Avalon/Starstock/Photoshot, 177. CBW/Alamy Stock Photo, 179-180. Mirrorpix, 181. Embassy/Laurence Turman/REX/Shutterstock, 182. Avalon/UPPA/Photoshot, 183. Keystone USA/REX/Shutterstock (top), 183. Mirrorpix (bottom), 184. Michael Putland/Getty Images,185. Mirrorpix, 186. NASA, 187. AFP/Getty Images (top left), 187. AP/Press Association Images (top right), 187 (bottom) AFP/Getty Images

Every effort has been made to acknowledge correctly and contact the source and/or copyright holder of each picture and Carlton Books Limited apologises for any unintentional errors or omissions that will be corrected in future editions of this book.

PUBLISHING CREDITS

Editorial Manager: Roland Hall
Design Manager: Russell Knowles
Design: James Pople
Picture Manager: Steve Behan
Production: Sarah Kramer